Understanding the Times of CHRIST

William W. Menzies

Developed and Edited by the
National Sunday School Department

Gospel Publishing House
Springfield, Missouri

02–0622

Library of Congress Catalog Card Number 91–70704
International Standard Book Number 0–88243–622–8
Printed in the United States of America

Contents

Contents

Preface

The Assemblies of God have been a people of The Book from the beginning. Our Fellowship has joined rank with other evangelicals from the time of the Reformation in declaring boldly that we take the Scriptures very, very seriously. Without apology we lay claim to the conservative, "grammatico-historical" interpretation of the Word of God, by which we mean that the words themselves are inerrant, and that they must be seen in the historical setting in which they were uttered to be properly interpreted. The historical aspect of this approach is the burden of this volume. The assignment has been to capture in a few brief pages as much as possible of the situation of the times of Christ, who is the center, not only of the Bible, but of all history.

The writer is deeply indebted to numerous authors whose works he has referred to constantly. In consultation with the editors it was agreed that footnotes would be virtually omitted, not to suggest that all the ideas are the writer's own, but for the purpose of aiding the reader to move with greater ease through the text. Special acknowledgment is due Dr. Stanley Horton who has read the manuscript and offered numerous helpful suggestions.

An entire chapter has been devoted to a description of the Qumran community. This has been deemed to be advisable inasmuch as recent archaeological discoveries have catapulted this little known group into front-page news for two decades now. It is important that those who teach in our Sunday schools have some awareness of the issues involved.

The writer sincerely trusts that those who read this volume will come to a deeper appreciation for, and stronger kinship with, Jesus Christ, whose times are after all not limited to first-century Palestine, but continue world without end.

WILLIAM W. MENZIES

1

Before the Time of Christ

Events in the last years of the nations of Israel and Judah and in the twilight years between Malachi and Matthew are important for understanding the world into which Jesus was born. God was at work shaping the course of empires for the cradling of the Saviour. At the ripeness of time Jesus came.

The Exile

From the time of Abraham onward God had entered into a series of covenants with His chosen people. He had promised blessing in return for faithful obedience. He had also warned that judgment would befall the people should they dilute true worship with idolatrous practices. Much of the Old Testament story is the disclosure of the sorrowing Father grieving over the recurring waywardness of His disobedient children. When at last the cup of Israel's iniquity had overflowed, God's wrath descended upon them. The Northern Kingdom, arrogant and prosperous in the middle-eighth century B.C., heedless of the pleadings of prophets like Amos and Hosea, fell victim to the conquering armies of Assyria. Samaria, the capital, was subjugated in 721 B.C., just a bare generation from the days of relative prosperity and optimism. In harmony with the prevailing practice of ancient empires the Assyrians deported many of the most capable people, thereby weakening the subjugated country beyond recovery. The shattered Northern Kingdom would not rise again.

To the south, Judah had the advantage of Israel's bitter experience to reinforce the warnings of faithful prophets. But apart from the brief revival in the days of good King Josiah, Judah seemed bent on pursuing a collision course with divine judgment. The pleadings of Nahum, Zephaniah, Habakkuk, and Jeremiah were largely ignored. Mighty Babylon, its star of empire rising, became God's means for chastening Judah. A series of three deportations to Babylon between 605 B.C. and 586 B.C. virtually destroyed Judah. The period of the Hebrew monarchy was at an end, and a watershed in the history of God's people had been reached.

The exiles from Judah fared reasonably well in Babylon at first. They had considerable personal liberty and opportunity to prosper economically. Still, they chafed under foreign domination; they longed for their homeland. The prophets Ezekiel, Obadiah, and Daniel proved to be a source of great encouragement to the people of God, pointing them to coming deliverance.

The Restoration

Deliverance came, but from a most unexpected quarter. The fortunes of empire changed swiftly in the sixth century B.C. Nabonidus, successor to Nebuchadnezzar, had become increasingly concerned over the military successes of Cyrus, an Elamite king. In spite of elaborate defenses erected at Babylon by Belshazzar, oldest son and regent of Nabonidus, the reins of empire passed to Cyrus, now master of all Medo-Persia, in 539 B.C. Babylon's glory was brilliant but brief. In Babylon, the Jews rejoiced at this change in affairs, for conditions for them had grown increasingly more severe under Nabonidus.

In his first year as monarch, Cyrus, without doubt prompted by God, issued the famous decree, not only permitting but encouraging the Jews to return to their native land. How wonderfully God had intervened in behalf of His chastened people! Had not Isaiah predicted this deliverance 150 years before? Now, under the leadership of Zerubbabel, prince of Judah, and Joshua, descendant of the priests, more than 42,000 exiles trekked westward to their homeland. Although it may appear that this was a large contingent, most of the exiles remained in Babylon. Thus only a remnant actually returned to Palestine.

The company that returned concentrated in the area immediately surrounding Jerusalem. Their immediate objective, after erecting shelters for themselves, was the restoration of the Temple, which had been destroyed by Nebuchadnezzar in 586 B.C. Amid shouts of jubilation the work was undertaken in 536 B.C. Initial enthusiasm gave way to despair, however, and the work lagged for sixteen years. Cyrus had died in 529 B.C., and imperial policy toward the Jews seems to have changed. The local inhabitants were hostile, but, more than all, the people themselves had become afflicted with greed and apathy.

Into this dismal situation, God sent two mouthpieces, the prophets Zechariah and Haggai. Their fresh message caused the people to repent, and the work was undertaken with renewed vigor. In the meantime, a second benefactor, in the person of Darius, appeared on the scene. Darius had come to leadership of the Medo-Persian empire in 522 B.C. He issued a fresh proclamation, which not only reinforced the forgotten desire of Cyrus for the displaced Jews, but even added funds from the state treasury for the expediting of the rebuilding of their Temple. So, the work rapidly progressed, and the Temple at last was dedicated in 516 B.C., just 70 years after it had been destroyed!

Little is known of the sixty years following the rebuilding of the Temple. The Book of Esther fits this period, but reflects Jewish life in the Persian capital, far to the east, rather than life in Palestine.

One might have hoped that the erection of the new Temple would mark a new golden age for Jewish national life, but the picture is unhappily quite the reverse. Beset by hostile neighbors in Palestine, discouraged by periodic oppressive imperial policies, and afflicted by weaknesses of internal leadership, the Jews found their dream of a reestablished Davidic monarchy was not yet to be realized. Symbolic of this disappointed hope is the lackluster Zerubbabel, the last of the princes. Political power was passing increasingly into the hands of the priesthood, a priesthood bent on accommodation to the local Palestinian culture. Intermarriage with unbelievers was the occasion for introducing a whole host of evils. This spirit of compromise led to a marked deterioration in the spiritual life of the people.

God raised up a special instrument to call the people to spiritual renewal. Ezra, of priestly lineage and a capable leader, had the advantage of influence in the Persian court for He was held in high esteem by Artaxerxes. When news came to Ezra of the deterioration of spiritual conditions in Palestine, he laid out the matter before the emperor. Artaxerxes dispatched Ezra on a special mission, accompanied by a fresh wave of Jewish emigrants and armed with a royal decree. The new treaty gave large powers to Ezra to refurbish the Temple, but more than that, to restore the purity of worship to the people of God. In 458 B.C., Ezra arrived on the scene as God's Reformer. When he saw the wretched conditions for himself, he cried out in anguish for his people (Ezra 9). Ezra's reform was deeply spiritual. He led the people in prayer, in confession, and in repudiation of the evils into which they had fallen, "according to the law" (Ezra 10:3). It was a Biblical revival, centered in the proclamation of the Word of God. Fourteen years later, at the dedication of the walls that were erected under the able leadership of Governor Nehemiah, Ezra again led the nation in a solemn consecration to the Law of the Lord (Nehemiah 10). How different things might have been for God's people if they had not forgotten to walk with God and to obey His Word!

Once again as Malachi, the last of the Old Testament prophets, writes about the year 400 B.C., one sees the recurrence of the oft-repeated pattern in Jewish national life. The evils of spiritual skepticism and indifference again creep like a shadow across the troubled land. It is with a portent of further chastening that the Old Testament prophecies come to a conclusion.

The Greek Rule (332–168 B.C.)

Alexander. Crowned King of Macedonia at 20, Alexander in

a series of decisive victories became master of the Near East, including the Persian Empire. Victories at Troy, Issus, Arbela, Tyre, and Gaza between 334 and 332 B.C. virtually annihilated resistance. Jerusalem surrendered to Alexander in 332 B.C. After reigning but a dozen years, the youthful empire-builder died in Babylon, dreaming of pressing the borders of empire to India and beyond. The meteoric career of this remarkable general had strategic significance for the Church Age to come. The spread of the Greek language throughout the Mediterranean basin and the encouragement that Alexander and his followers gave to Jewish colonization throughout the empire in time became the highways over which the Gospel was carried.

The Diadochoi. Alexander's death precipitated a long struggle among his generals for the fruits of conquest. The "Diadochoi," as Alexander's successors were called, did not satisfactorily resolve this struggle until 301 B.C., when by common agreement the empire was divided four ways. Even then the peace that was secured was uneasy, being broken periodically by open warfare. Only two of the realms thus created by the division of Alexander's empire are of importance to Palestinian history. One center of power was Egypt, where the Greek general Ptolemy I founded a dynasty that was to last until Roman times. The Ptolemies of Egypt dominated Palestine, with but brief interruptions, from the time of Alexander's death until the beginning of the second century B.C. To the north of Palestine, the other center of power was Syria, a realm dominated by the Seleucid Dynasty. Hapless Palestine lay between these great powers, a pawn on the chessboard of international politics.

Life Under the Ptolemies. For one hundred years, the Jews, both in Egypt and Palestine, enjoyed a period of quiet and relative prosperity. These early Ptolemies were more concerned with literary pursuits than with military matters. Beginning with Ptolemy Philopater (221–204 B.C.), however, a drastic change occurred. While on a tour of his provinces following a successful campaign against the Seleucid king of Syria, Antiochus III, Philopater attempted to force his way into the Temple's inner sanctuary in Jerusalem. According to tradition he was smitten with a kind of paralysis, and on his return to Alexandria launched a repressive program aimed at the Jews.

Seleucid Oppression. Upon the death of Philopater, Antiochus renewed his assault on Palestine. The Jews, very likely because of the cruelty of Philopater, favored the invading Syrian army. After a series of battles, culminating in the rout of the Egyptians at the decisive battle at Paneas in the Jordan Valley in 198 B.C., Palestine came under the dominion of the Seleucid rulers. The Jews, weary of an apparently endless succession of armies crossing and recrossing their devastated land, hoped for relief. Instead of tranquility, the next years would be marked by even greater turmoil and violence. Daniel prophesies at the closing years of Seleucid rule over Palestine in language that appears to be descriptive of the terror of Antichrist's rule (Daniel 11, 12).

Because of a series of disastrous military adventures against the Romans the Syrians were reduced to the level of tax-gatherers, having huge war debts to repay to Rome. In desperation the Syrians resorted to the sacking of temples and levying heavy taxes on the peoples of their realm. An additional distress inflicted on the Jews was the Syrian policy of enforced Hellenization. During the period of the Ptolemaic supremacy, large numbers of Jews had gone to Egypt, many settling in Alexandria and enjoying a degree of harmony with the local Greek-speaking populace. However, their "Hellenization" was by choice, and did not involve the abrogation of their spiritual heritage. But, with the coming of the Seleucids, Greek customs and philosophy were imposed as part of the Syrian policy for Palestine. The priesthood, who served as the official representatives of the people, were the ones who primarily dealt with the foreign governing authorities who controlled the land. Unfortunately, it was the priesthood in Jerusalem which seemed to take an important part in the encouragement of the Hellenization of the land. The last genuine high priest, Onias, had his office taken from him by his treacherous brother, Jason, who purchased the claim to that title with a large sum of money which he agreed to pay to the Seleucid tyrant in power. Jason also agreed to promote Greek fashions and learning, and to build a gymnasium for the Greek games. The attendance of the priests at the games and at the adjoining race track was a great abomination to most of the people, for these occasions were opened by invocations to pagan deities. Foremost in the conservative reaction against the temporizing policies of the Jerusalem priests were the Hasidim, the Pious, the forerunners of the Essenes of Jesus' day. But already the priesthood was dominated by the rationalistic element who were precursors of the Sadducees. The attempt to compel the Jews to adopt Greek polytheism reached its most agonizing dimensions in the reign of Antiochus IV, the despot whom Daniel pictures as the epitome of what Antichrist shall be.

Antiochus IV came to power in the Seleucid dynasty in 175 B.C. He assumed the grand title of Epiphanes, "the Illustrious One," but his reputation for cruelty and his devious behavior caused many to nickname him Epimanes, "the Madman." His vicious assault on Judea is a well-documented illustration of the barbarity of his nature. In 169 B.C. Antiochus launched an abortive invasion against his archfoe, Egypt. Frustrated in his attempt to conquer the land, he vented his rage on the city of Jerusalem as his defeated army trudged homeward through Judea. He gained possession of the city through trickery, sacked and burned it in a senseless outpouring of rage. The result was 40,000 citizens massacred with perhaps an equal number sold into slavery. His mad objective seemed to be to convert or kill. Severe laws were swiftly decreed, aimed particularly at the Hasidim. The observance of the Sabbath, circumcision, even possessing the Hebrew Scriptures were made crimes punishable by death. Jewish worship was outlawed, and pagan altars were erected in cities and hamlets throughout Judea. These repressive decrees were enforced with unbelievable ferocity.

The final outrage was the sacking of the Temple and the erection of an idol on the altar in honor of Zeus. On December 25, 168 B.C., Antiochus offered to the pagan deity a sow on the altar, an act of sacrilege and blasphemy referred to by Daniel

as "the abomination of desolation" (Daniel 11:31; 12:11). A reign
of terror reminiscent of the latter-day "time of Jacob's trouble"
had descended over the land.

The Maccabean Revolt (168–142 B.C.)

At first the Jews, particularly the Hasidim, suffered pas-
sively. Some were massacred, without offering resistance, rather
than break the Sabbath. The breaking point came at the village
of Modin, a few miles northwest of Jerusalem. The Syrian com-
missioner had come to enforce public sacrifice to the pagan
gods. When one of the local citizens stepped to the altar to
comply, the aged priest Mattathias, in a burst of passionate
zeal, killed both the temporizing Jew and the government agent
and proceeded to break down the pagan altar. The old priest
and his five sons, together with their families, fled into the
Judean wilderness. For a year the old priest led a band of
guerrillas who attacked by night, destroying pagan altars and
discomfiting the Syrian garrison. Upon the death of the old
priest, the leadership of the growing guerrilla band was be-
queathed to the third son, Judas, who had earned the nickname
Maccabeus, "the Hammer."

Under the leadership of Judas, possibly the greatest military
genius in Jewish history, the Jewish patriots carried on a successful guerrilla war against the despised Syrians. He succeeded in bringing the Syrian army, dispatched by Antiochus
to quell the rebellion, to terms of truce. This made it possible
for the Jews to rededicate the polluted Temple, just three years
after the desecration by Antiochus. A feast was instituted to
commemorate the cleansing of the Temple and the restoration
of religious liberty, a feast still observed as Hanukkah, or "the
Feast of Lights."

Although their immediate objective of religious toleration
had been won, Judas and his guerrilla band raised their sights
to the larger objective of national independence. Warfare lin-
gered on for years. In 160 B.C. Judas fell in battle. His younger
brother Jonathan, now the high priest, assumed direction of

the campaign. Upon the death of Jonathan, the leadership passed to the last son of Mattathias, Simon. In 142 B.C the Syrians finally wearied of the struggle and granted independence to Judea. Thus was added to the pages of Jewish history a heroic chapter still fondly retold to oncoming generations. After 400 years of foreign bondage, the Jews at last were free!

The Hasmonean Rule (142–63 B.C.)[1]

Relative tranquility on the borders gave hopeful promise to the newly freed nation. However, internal political struggles beset the Jews almost from the start. By the time independence had been achieved, the people were divided into two camps. The original supporters of the Maccabean revolt were interested only in religious freedom. They withdrew from the struggle after the cleansing of the Temple. The party later to be known as the Pharisees belonged to this group. The other faction was interested in political power, and it was their support of the later Maccabean priest-generals that swept them into influence when independence came. These people, later developing into the Sadducee party, controlled the priesthood.

Since the real political power in Jewish society was the priesthood, its control became the object of ambition of various factions and individuals. Simon the high priest was brutally murdered with two of his sons by his own son-in-law, Ptolemy. Eventually, the remaining son of Simon, John Hyrcanus, was able to bring a degree of stability to the priesthood, lasting for thirty years until his death in 104 B.C. After the death of John Hyrcanus, dissensions between the various political parties brought the country to virtual civil war. These years are a sordid tangle of family plots, counterplots and assassinations. Weakened by domestic chaos, Judea became an easy target for the growing ambition of Rome, whose interest in the Near East had been growing. Independence, so nobly won, was destined to be brief.

The Roman Era (63 B.C.–)

The Romans, under the skillful Pompey, had been closing in

on Syria and neighboring states. In the midst of the civil disorder in Judea, it appears that various factions sent delegations to Damascus to negotiate for Roman favor. John Hyrcanus II, lineal descendant of the Maccabees, high priest and self-styled king of Judea, was given the nod by Pompey. He surrendered Jerusalem to the Roman general, and in return for other political favors Hyrcanus, although stripped of the title of king, was appointed ethnarch of Judea. Dissident elements in Judea were vanquished, stability had returned to the troubled land, but at the cost of their hard-won freedom.

The Jews were once again a subjugated people. Judea was formally annexed to the Roman banner, and the people were required to pay tribute. It was a kind of twilight existence, for until 37 B.C. the Romans allowed the Jews to have their own rulers. Even the limited autonomy they had enjoyed during the first years of Roman occupation was choked off by the imposition of a man of Roman choosing to be their leader, Herod the Great.

The wry twist is that Herod the Great was a descendant of the Idumeans whom John Hyrcanus had conquered in the previous century. He was a brutal man, guilty of murdering two wives, three sons, and other relatives; yet he was recognized as an able administrator by the Romans. The Jews resisted the Roman announcement in 40 B.C. that this hated Idumean should be their "king," and for three years Herod had to wage virtual war on Judea to make real what the Romans had enacted into law. By 37 B.C. Herod was ensconced in Jerusalem and was in fact the king of Judea, a puppet of Rome. The Palestinian area was now fully Roman territory, controlled by their own appointee, and subject to the immediate oversight of the governor of Syria. The transition to Roman control was now complete.

Summary

In the years immediately preceding the Incarnation the people of God could look back upon their history and there recall a succession of national disasters, the gloom punctuated but briefly by occasional glimmerings of light. These brief glimmerings were a portent of the promise given to the fathers of old that a Deliverer should come. In their despair, there was a heightened sense of expectancy regarding the promise of a Messiah.

---

[1]The family name of Mattathias was apparently Hasmon, thus the dynasty was known as *Hasmonean.*

2

Palestinian Politics

In the Biblical record of the trial of Jesus, three different types of governmental authority are apparent. Jesus first is summoned before the high priest (Luke 22:54). Then He appears before the Roman governor, Pilate (Luke 23:1). During the course of the governor's dealings with Him, Jesus is arraigned before Herod Antipas (Luke 23:7). These three basic types of authority form the political background of the New Testament story.

At the risk of oversimplification, one may view these as three concentric circles. The outer circle may represent the naked Roman presence, the Roman governors or procurators, who were called into areas demanding special emergency oversight, such as Judea in the days of Jesus. The next circle represents the long-range program of the Romans, a diplomatic solution to the governing of a subjugated people. This was the Herodian family. The Herods, who derived their authority from Rome, were imposed upon the people, but it was hoped by the Romans that the people would accept the Herodian family as their kings. The inner circle represents the ongoing daily life of the people, which was supervised by the high priesthood under limits prescribed by Rome. The danger of oversimplification lies in the fact that Palestine in the first century was divided into several distinct regions. It was primarily in Judea, the Jewish heartland, that the Roman military governors operated during the lifetime of Christ. The Herodian family controlled the other provinces of Palestine during those years, but there was no Herod in Judea from A.D. 6 until A.D. 41. From A.D. 44 until the revolution of A.D. 66, which led to the destruction of the nation, there were Roman governors operating contemporaneously with the Herodian family throughout Palestine. Meanwhile, the high priesthood had a continuous history until the destruction of the Temple in A.D. 70. Let us begin our story with the Herodian family.

The Herods

Herod the Great (37–4 B.C.). Although Herod succeeded in getting the Romans to appoint him King of Judea in 40 B.C., it took three years to subjugate the unwilling population. His actual reign began in 37 B.C. However, his work had only begun. Twelve additional years were expended in attempting to consolidate his hold on the throne. The persistent threat to his authority was the Hasmonean spirit. Of the two parties that were emerging in the religio-political life of the Jews, the Sadducees with their political ambitions were most closely allied to the later Hasmoneans. Thus of necessity Herod allied himself to the Pharisees. It was in his lifetime that they enjoyed their greatest flowering. Not until Herod's death were the Sadducees to recover their earlier supremacy, a supremacy which prevailed during the life and ministry of Christ.

One of Herod's first acts was to slaughter 45 of the leading Sadducee leaders in Jerusalem. In their stead he promoted Pharisee leaders, for his shrewdness told him that the Pharisees were not interested in politics and would not pose a threat to his ambitions. His interest in the Pharisees was not out of religious conviction; Herod was more Roman than Jewish. His real desire was to weld Roman paganism to Judaism. As an indication of his religious outlook, he utterly disregarded the hereditary character of the high-priestly office, appointing and removing men at will and without regard to any principle other than their usefulness to his personal ambitions. He also spent lavishly on adorning pagan temples, even outside the borders of his own kingdom. To be sure, he did much to help the Palestinian Jews in a material way. But even this seems to have been motivated by opportunism, for he had to discover ways of getting a resentful populace to accept him as their ruler.

Manipulating the priesthood was not sufficient to remove doubts about possible political rivals for Herod. A few of the Hasmonean family still survived. Because of the current temper of politics he with reluctance appointed Aristobulus, a Hasmonean, as high priest. Aristobulus, although only a boy of 16, was received with such acclaim that Herod became extremely jealous of him. Herod invited Aristobulus to a feast and had him drowned in a manner which appeared to be an accident. After this cruel murder, one by one the remaining Hasmoneans were executed, including his Hasmonean wife, Mariamne, the one woman whom he apparently really loved. He was filled with remorse for some time after her death. By the year 25 B.C., the last heirs-apparent of the Hasmonean family had been disposed of and the crown of Herod was finally secured.

The next dozen years were the years of greatest achievement for Herod. His most significant contribution was in the area of building. At first he built only fortresses, but before long entire cities on a grand scale were planned and built. The military construction provided a successful wall of defense against external invasion, and provided for the garrisoning of Roman troops within the country to quell possible insurrection. Representative of the fortresses and garrisoned cities of Herod's day was Caesarea, the great Roman seaport and military bastion on the Mediterranean. There, along a coast without much in the way of hospitable harbors, Herod had built over a period of twelve years a magnificent seawall, overlooked by a great temple dedicated to Caesar. A theater, amphitheater, and a great marketplace added to the splendor of Caesarea.

However, in spite of the introduction of Roman gymnasia, racetracks, theaters, and other features of pagan life, Herod the diplomat recognized that he had to attempt to win the Jews in addition to ingratiating himself with the Romans. To do this, he conceived the idea of rebuilding the ancient Temple in Jerusalem. This monumental enterprise was to be his crowning achievement. Zerubbabel's Temple never had the grandeur and glory of that of Solomon. It had always been something of a disappointment to the Jews. Herod planned to follow the basic pattern of the earlier temples, but on a scale even grander than Solomon's. One thousand priests were trained as artisans, so that no profane hands should be involved in the work—a concession to the Jews who were suspicious of Herod and his motives. The work did not begin until the materials and workmen were assembled. Huge blocks of white marble were brought to the city to the building site. The work on the Temple itself began in 20 B.C. and although it was largely completed by the time of the death of Herod, work was still in progress in the days of Christ. In spite of this great effort, Herod never really won the people. He was still an Idumean, a foreigner, and his support of pagan temples and activities unmasked his basic lack of true spirituality. He was not a Jew at heart, and the people knew it.

Herod was an international opportunist. This was an important key to his lengthy rule. During his years as ruler of Judea, numerous colossal changes had taken place in the world of Roman politics. Almost uncannily the crafty Herod was able to switch allegiances to rival powers at opportune moments, thus avoiding the wreckage of fallen leadership. He was a diplomatic genius, able to consolidate his hold on the throne by pruning away possible rivals within the kingdom, and by adroitly switching loyalties to the great powers in the Roman world.

Insatiable ambition and constant double-dealing, however, eventually caught up with this conscienceless potentate. The last years of his life were miserable and tormented. Intrigue and jealousy filled the royal court. In an inhuman act of unbelievable barbarity, Herod condemned to death his own sons, the two children of his murdered wife Mariamne, whom he feared were plotting to take his crown. Another son, Antipater, who had in fact been plotting against his father, was also executed.

Matthew 2:1–18 tells of the visit of the Wise Men from the East to Judea at the time of Christ's infancy. The treachery with which Herod dealt with them fits the character he displayed on other occasions. The massacre of the children of Bethlehem was an act not at all out of harmony with the ruthlessness with which he managed his own household.

Five days after his son Antipater was executed, the aged, miserable king died, evidently of intestinal cancer. For all the stimulus to the economy and prosperity of his realm he may have brought, Herod's name must be considered "Great" for wickedness as well as worldly achievements.

Upon the death of Herod, Caesar Augustus divided the Palestinian area among three surviving sons of Herod. To Archelaus was given the jurisdiction of the southern region, consisting of Judea, Samaria, and Idumea. To Philip was given the control of the region to the north of the Sea of Galilee and east of Jordan, in the most remote area, quite removed from the center of the activity of the New Testament story. The region of Galilee and Perea was given to Antipas, the Herod most frequently mentioned in the story of Jesus.

Archelaus. When Herod died in 4 B.C., there was already considerable popular discontent in Judea. Augustus refused to give any of Herod's sons the title of king, because of the insecurity in the realm. To Archelaus was given the lesser title of ethnarch.

Archelaus proved to be the most controversial of Herod's sons. He continued his father's program of encouraging public building enterprises, but in spite of this public-spirited activity, his personal life and ruthless repression of dissident elements gained him the ill will of the domain. He married Glaphyra, wife of his half-brother, divorcing his own wife in order to do so. This outraged the Jews. Then, during the Passover season, a rebellion broke out in Jerusalem. To quell this uprising, Archelaus sent in troops who killed three thousand citizens, many of whom were innocent pilgrims visiting the city. So, at the outset of his reign, Archelaus developed a reputation for terror and arrogance. It is little wonder that when Joseph heard that Archelaus was ruler over Judea, he feared to take Jesus and Mary there, preferring instead to go to Galilee (Matthew 2:22).

In the ninth year of his reign, a delegation of leading men from Judea and Samaria went to Rome to protest the reign of terror of Archelaus. Augustus, noted for his concern over the welfare of the far-flung and varied peoples within his Empire, listened with patience, and decided in their favor. Augustus deposed Archelaus, banished him to Gaul, and confiscated his fortune. Temporarily the region of Judea, Samaria, and Idumea was put directly under the control of a military governor. It would not be until after the death and resurrection of Jesus that Herods again would appear on the Judean scene.

Philip. To Philip was given the outermost region of Palestine, and a title to match. The term tetrarch was of lesser dignity than ethnarch. The population was less Jewish and more Greek-speaking than the rest of Palestine, except for the region known as Decapolis, which bordered Philip's territory on the south. Philip's rule was quite unlike that of the Herods in general. It was quiet and peaceful. Like his father, he gained fame as a builder. An important contribution was the reconstruction of the ancient city of Panias, renamed Caesarea Philippi in honor of Augustus and to distinguish it from the great seaport built by his father. Matthew 16:13 cites the only instance when Jesus ventured north from Galilee into the district of Caesarea Philippi. Evidently the Gentile composition of the people living in Philip's jurisdiction did not fit into Jesus' concern to begin first with His own people. That He did not entirely exclude ministry to Gentiles, as evidenced by the visit to Caesarea Philippi, lets one see that Jesus has compassion for all men.

Philip died in A.D. 34. For three years the territory was administered through the office of the Syrian military governor, but in A.D. 37 it was made part of Herod Agrippa's realm.

Antipas. The Herod most often mentioned by the Bible writers is Herod Antipas, tetrarch of Galilee and Perea. His reign lasted until A.D. 39, during which he distinguished himself as the most able of the sons of Herod. The chief monument to his building program was the city of Tiberias, a capital he erected on the southwest shore of the Sea of Galilee in A.D. 22 in honor of the Emperor Tiberius.

Evidence that Herod Antipas displayed a scheming character

is the reference by Jesus to him as "that fox" (Luke 13:31). His defective character led eventually to his downfall. Antipas had married a daughter of Aretas, king of the Nabatean Arabs, whose capital was the secluded city of Petra in the Dead Sea wilderness. On a visit to Rome, Antipas stayed with a half-brother, Herod Philip (not the same as the tetrarch, however). He became enamored of Herodias, the wife of Philip during the visit. He divorced his wife and married Herodias, but succeeded in incurring the displeasure of the prophet John the Baptist. John fearlessly denounced the illegal union, and gained the ill will of Herodias and her daughter Salome, who had joined Herod at the palace in Tiberias. Evidently Antipas respected the courage of John, but persuaded by his wife and daughter, he had John beheaded (Mark 6:17–29). Josephus, the historian, indicates that Antipas was afraid that the great public following of John might develop into revolt.

Retribution came after John's death. The deposed wife had fled to her father, Aretas. Outraged by the insult to his daughter, Aretas declared war on Antipas and inflicted heavy losses on him. Evidently in the course of the campaign Antipas had made a pact with the Parthians, whom the Romans hated. In A.D. 29, Herodias goaded Antipas into appealing to Emperor Caligula for advancement from tetrarch to king, but when news reached Rome of the alliance he had made with the Parthians, Caligula not only did not grant him his wish, but banished him to Gaul and gave his realm to Herod Agrippa I.

Herod Antipas entered the life of Jesus on more than one occasion. He had a deep sense of guilt over the murder of John the Baptist, and feared that Jesus was John risen from the dead (Matthew 14:1, 2). Herod later was present in Jerusalem at the time of the trial of Jesus. Pilate, the military governor of Judea, learning that Jesus was from Galilee and therefore subject to Antipas, sent him to Herod for judgment. Herod seems to have been curious to see Jesus, of whom he had heard so much, wishing to see a miracle. Disappointed that Jesus would not perform for him, Antipas loosed his men to treat Jesus with indignities and contempt (Luke 23:6–12). He then would accept no further responsibility for him, returning him to Pilate. So, the Herod who had the greatest opportunity to know Jesus Christ, spurned that opportunity, not recognizing the Son of God standing in his presence.

The Later Herods. "Herod the king," referred to in Acts 12:1 as a persecutor of the apostles, was Herod Agrippa I. Agrippa was a son of Aristobulus, a Hasmonean, and a grandson of Herod the Great. He was brought up in Rome and except for brief periods lived much of his life there. With the accession of Caligula to the imperial throne, Agrippa came into considerable importance. In A.D. 32 Caligula made him king of the territory that had belonged to Herod Philip. And, when Antipas fell into disfavor and was banished, Galilee and Perea were added to his domain, this taking place two years after he had been first named king. When Claudius became emperor in A.D. 41, he added further to the territory of Agrippa's kingdom, giving to him Judea and Samaria. By this time Agrippa's control extended to almost the same limits as did that of his grandfather Herod the Great.

Agrippa was able to curry the favor of the Jews more successfully than did his predecessors, partially because of his Hasmonean ancestry, but also because he advocated practices that pleased the Jews. For example, during the reign of Caligula he headed off an imminent revolt by persuading Caligula not to erect a statue of himself in the Jerusalem Temple. Personally, he identified with the Jews more than the other Herods, worshipping regularly in the Temple, and keeping the Law with zeal. His Jewish sympathies very likely account for his determined persecution of the apostles recorded in Acts 12. He sought to aid the Pharisees in their growing struggle with the rising sect known as Christians. He killed James, the brother of John, and arrested Peter in an attempt to harass and intimidate the fledgling church. How wonderful that God so miraculously delivered Peter out of the clutches of this enemy of Christ (Acts 12:5–17).

The policy of the Herods was to mediate between Rome and the interests of the Jews. Herod Agrippa, although a far more zealous Jew religiously than any of the others of the clan, nonetheless continued the policy of truckling to Rome. Evidence of this is his attendance at the Roman games at Caesarea at a festive occasion in A.D. 44 in honor of the emperor. Evidently his robes glistening in the sun caused people to murmur that it was the voice of a god who spoke (Acts 12:22). Luke, the writer of Acts, records that Agrippa's failure to honor God on that occasion resulted in immediate retribution. Josephus records that within a week he was dead of a loathsome intestinal disease. The sudden death of Herod interrupted the kingdom for six years, for the only son of Agrippa was too young to be entrusted by the Romans with the regal authority. About A.D. 50, however, young Herod Agrippa II assumed the responsibility of the kingdom during the time when Claudius was emperor.

Herod Agrippa II is best known for his encounter with Paul (Acts 25:13 to 26:32). The occasion was the accession of Festus to the office of military governor of Judea. King Herod, in company with his sister Bernice who served as his royal consort, went to the Roman headquarters at Caesarea to welcome the new governor. The governor, being a pagan, had no knowledge of how to handle the Jewish prisoner, Paul, who had been held in custody in the military prison at Caesarea since the threatened lynching in Jerusalem (Acts 23: 12–35). Herod, although not as religious a Jew as his father, nonetheless knew something of Jewish customs, and served as legal advisor to Festus regarding Paul while he and his sister were visiting in Caesarea.

The last issue of significance regarding the Herods was the role Agrippa II played in the great rebellion that erupted in Palestine in A.D. 66. He tried unsuccessfully to prevent the outbreak of war, but being unable to keep peace, he threw his lot in with the Romans. For his allegiance to Rome his reward was the enlargement of his kingdom. Agrippa II died childless in the year 100. And so came to an end the strange dynasty of the Herodian family, kings who never really had more than the status of Roman puppets, nor the loyalty of the Jews whom they ruled. Theirs was in truth a twilight kingdom.

The Roman Governors

Judea was an especially turbulent area difficult for the Romans to manage. Archelaus, through his unwise policies, had brought Judea almost to open revolt. When in A.D. 6, Caesar Augustus deposed Archelaus, he replaced the Herodian line in Judea with a series of military governors called procurators. This move indicates the sense of urgent need for more direct military oversight. In the Roman imperial system, procurator was the title given to governors of less significant provinces. In Judea the procurators were responsible to the more important Roman governor of Syria, the imperial legate. However, within that framework, the governors of Judea did have troops at their disposal, and had the oversight of the military control of the province, as well as the care of the financial management. The seat of government of the procurators was Caesarea, in the palace of Herod (Acts 23:35). Ordinarily they came to Jerusalem only on the occasion of the great Jewish festivals, to keep order during which time they occupied Herod's palace on the west side of the city. The procurators collected the taxes, which the Sanhedrin was required to raise, together with the tolls and customs that the publicans gathered, and dispatched these funds to Caesar's treasury in Rome. The people were painfully aware of the advent of a new procurator, for the new ones were the ardent tax-collectors. Judeans knew well the significance of the term, "Render unto Caesar" (Matthew 22:21). And the procurators changed frequently. Of the nearly twenty that served Judea (and later all of Palestine) in the first century, the New Testament records only three.

In the year A.D. 26 Pilate was commissioned by the Emperor Tiberius to be the fifth procurator of Judea. He had about 120 cavalry troops and about 5,000 foot soldiers stationed with him at his headquarters at the coastal city of Caesarea, with a smaller detachment located at the fortress of Antonia near the

Temple in Jerusalem to serve as a garrison there. He had the power of life and death over the Judeans, and could reverse capital sentences handed down by the Sanhedrin. Such sentences had to be ratified by him. He appointed the high priests and even handled the Temple funds.

Pilate was not a good diplomat. He did various things that irritated the Jews unnecessarily. On one occasion he used money from the Temple treasury to build an aqueduct to carry water to the city. When Pilate, as was the custom, took up residence in Jerusalem at the time when pilgrims came to the great annual feasts, thousands of Jews rioted and demonstrated against this abuse. He turned his troops on the milling throng, with the result that a large number were killed. It is quite possible that this riot was fomented by the Galileans mentioned in Luke 13:1, 2. The fact that some of Herod Antipas' subjects from Galilee had been brutally killed by this high-handed treatment of the demonstrators may have been the reason that Pilate took pains to send Jesus to him for trial (Luke 23:6, 7).

A similar slaughter took place in Samaria at Pilate's behest, but the angered Samaritans sent a delegation to the imperial legate in Syria protesting Pilate's ruthless reign. Vitellius, the legate, ordered Pilate to answer for his actions to the emperor. Pilate was on his way to Rome when the Emperor Tiberius died (A.D. 37). There is a cloud of uncertainty over the last days of Pilate, but one tradition indicates that he was forced to commit suicide by the Romans.

Pilate is a tragic character. The New Testament record describing his role in the trial of Jesus depicts him as a weak character, ready to serve expediency rather than principle. He seems to have authorized the execution of Jesus, whom he knew to be innocent, more out of fear for his job—he was expected to keep the peace—than to please the Jewish leaders. The wording of the inscription he had placed on the cross indicates that he really was mocking the religious leaders (John 19:19–22).

Some critics have doubted the existence of Pilate as a historical figure. However, in 1961 a stone slab was discovered at Caesarea bearing his name along with that of Tiberius, supplying important archaeological confirmation for the Gospel record.

It is not until later in the New Testament story, during the ministry of Paul, that the other two procurators mentioned in the Bible appear on the scene. Felix served as procurator from A.D. 52 to 59. He was succeeded for two brief years by Festus. In the case of all three of these men, golden opportunity for obtaining life eternal stood in their presence, only to be rejected. How tragic was their spiritual darkness!

The Priesthood

Except for the years of exile, known as the Babylonian Captivity, the priesthood had served as the single most important controlling influence in the life of the people, for even in the days of the monarchy the kings recognized the priests to be spokesmen for God. With the rebuilding of Zerubbabel's Temple in 516 B.C., the priesthood took on an even more obvious role of political authority, for never again after this time would the concept of king be disconnected from the priestly office. With the Hasmoneans combining royalty and priesthood, the Jews never did accept the Roman-imposed Herodian kings as true kings. For them the real authority was the priesthood.

Both the Greek and Roman rulers of Palestine recognized the role of the priest in the life of the people. They were willing to give considerable liberty to the priests to administer the daily affairs of the people, as long as they did not interfere with concerns of foreign policy or attempt to undercut imperial control. With some notable lapses, such as the high-handed political appointments to the priestly office by some of the Herods, the high priest held office by hereditary right.

During the life of Christ, the priesthood was extremely powerful in Judea. The high priest on occasion brought pressure to bear on the Roman governor to secure a desired change in policy. One weapon in the arsenal of the priests was the influence they had on public opinion. "But the chief priests stirred up the multitude to ask him to release Barabbas for them instead" (Mark 15:11).

The high priest presided over the Sanhedrin, a powerful council of seventy elders, consisting of priests and other influential community leaders, forming a kind of religious aristocracy. This council, originating in the obscure past, possibly in Ezra's time, had by the time of Christ wide powers over the life of the people, an arrangement with which the Romans cooperated. The Sanhedrin exercised not only religious and civil authority, but also a limited criminal authority. It could order arrests by its own officers (see, for example, Matthew 26:47; Acts 4:1). It had power to sit as a court in judgment on offenses that were not capital crimes (Acts 4, 5). Judgment on capital crimes required the ratification of the Roman procurator (John 18:31), although the procurator usually acquiesced with the judgement of the Sanhedrin, for the people acknowledged the right of the Sanhedrin, according to Jewish law, to have the power of life and death (Matthew 26:66). The Romans, it seems, did reserve the right to interfere in any matter, if they deemed it necessary. An example is the story of Paul's arrest in Acts 23, in which the Romans spared Paul in spite of the Jewish authorities.

The activity of the Sanhedrin was according to a carefully worked out procedure, much of which, however, has not been preserved for us. It is known that they did not meet on festival days nor on the Sabbath. A defendant could be acquitted on the trial day, but one condemned could not be sentenced until the day following. In capital cases, one could argue for acquittal, but could not later change his mind. Should one, however, vote for condemnation, he was allowed to change his vote later. Acquittal required a simple majority vote; condemnation required a two-thirds vote. There was a clear attempt to prevent arbitrary judgment of the innocent. In view of this careful attempt to protect the innocent, there are numerous points in the trial of Jesus that are glaring breaches of the Sanhedrin's own concept of justice.

More will be said of the role of the priests in Palestinian

society later. It will be sufficient here to indicate the powerful role the priesthood had in the political life of the people.

Summary

It is within a framework of three kinds of government that the people in Jesus' day lived. Their daily life under the supervision of the priests continued much as it always had. The Roman presence came directly through the governors, and indirectly through the puppet-kings, the Herods.

3

Palestinian Judaism: Social Structures

Now we must be occupied with sketching the various groups of people that made up the society of Jesus' day. These were the people whom we meet in the pages of the Gospels, either directly or by inference. Who were they? What were they like? Perhaps if we spend these moments with people from the first century, it will help us to understand a little better why they did and said some of the things recorded in the New Testament. And it may encourage us to believe that Jesus is interested in meeting the needs of people today, who in reality are not very much different from the citizens of ancient Galilee and Judea.

The People of the Land

Socially the people of Palestine in the first century were quite divided. There was the sharp distinction between Jew and Gentile. Just as harsh a distinction was preserved between the religious and the nonreligious. Men and women were not considered on the same plane. There were sharp divisions over how much the people should bow to Rome. Perhaps most painful of all was the wall between the very rich and the very poor.

The aristocracy of Palestine was an interlocked web of economic power and religious power. The upper classes of society were *religious.* They tended to despise the poor who could not afford the luxury of observing the minute details of the Law. It is estimated that the poor constituted 90 percent of the population. The attitude of scorn and abhorrence manifested by the elite religious ruling classes is epitomized in the Pharisees, whose very name means *separate*. What a contrast was Jesus! Jesus took special pains to unmask the self-righteousness of those who drew their cloaks about them, lest they be contaminated by the *unclean* common people. He went out of His way to minister to the common people, and they heard the Good News of the Redeemer's love gladly.

The Pharisees taught that the people of the land, the Amhaarets, were not to be summoned as witnesses, nor their testimony admitted in law courts. Secrets were not to be entrusted to them. One of the poor could not even be appointed a guardian of an orphan. Intermarriage between the social aristocracy and the poor of the land was condemned as utterly abhorrent. Thus these peasants of the land suffered not only the cruel oppression of Roman taxation and tyranny, but also the haughty disdain of their own religious leaders.

Some of the people were so impoverished that they became slaves, a practice permitted by the Jewish Law. One or two years of poor crops or illness could easily reduce some of the poor to the status of slavery to richer landowners (Exodus 21:2, 3; Leviticus 25:39). However, the indentured servant, or bondman, had to be released after six years of servitude (Leviticus 25:40, 41). Life was so difficult that frequently the bondservant felt he would be better off than if he were on his own; some wished to continue on as more or less the outer fringe of the master's family. Some of these took an active and loyal interest in their master's business affairs (Luke 12:42–47). To leave the master's house was almost like leaving home, and one can detect the pathos of the slave in Jesus' parable when he faces the prospect of leaving (Luke 16:3).

The people did not live on the farms. They huddled together in villages, or if the village was large enough to merit a protecting wall, it was a town. From their village or town they went out to toil in the fields each day. Shopkeepers, peddlers, beggars, and householders mingled in the streets with farmers and shepherds. Matthew 21:33 refers to a tower in a vineyard. Such a tower was necessary at harvesttime to watch over the ripening crop, since the fields were left alone at night. The center of social activity for the poor of the land was the gate of the town or the village marketplace.

An important feature of the community life that helped to alleviate the strong class distinctions was the local synagogue, and the synagogue school for the boys. More will be said about the synagogue in a later chapter.

Let us now turn to a discussion of some of the important religious and religio-political groups of Jesus' day.

The Pharisees

Of the total population of a half-million Jews living in Palestine in the first century, only about 6,000 adult males were members of the sect of the Pharisees. It is apparent that they had an influence out of all proportion to their numbers in the time of Jesus. After the destruction of the Temple in A.D. 70, they alone of the Jewish religious parties survived, forming the basis of what is today modern orthodox Judaism. The Pharisees form an important link in our chain of understanding.

The origin of the Pharisees is hidden in obscurity. It is generally believed that they were the successors of the strict Jews in the Greek period who resisted the Hellenizing process. In the Seleucid era these conservative Jews were known as the Hasidim, "the righteous ones." When the first phase of the Maccabean struggle resulted in the successful restoration of the religious freedom the Jews so ardently desired, most of the Hasidim withdrew from further political controversy. The Maccabees shifted the struggle from a quest for religious freedom to a struggle for national independence, but many religious people lost interest. The name Pharisee first appears during the reign of priest-king John Hyrcanus late in the second century B.C. They got this name, meaning "separate," likely because they disapproved of the prevailing practice of the high-priesthood. These Hasidim who withdrew from public life turned their attention to religious matters, feeling that the solution to the national problems would not come about through political means. Their religious zeal found expression in explicit obedience to the oral and the written law. Scrupulous behavior characterized the average Pharisee.

Their rigorous practices were founded on the Old Testament. However, they put great weight on the oral tradition of some of their great teachers, and in this way built a rather sizable code of laws to govern the details of daily behavior. They practiced ritualistic prayer and fasting, together with other rites of purification. Tithing of their property was attended with legalistic care (Matthew 23:23). The Sabbath was safeguarded by a variety of limitations, which they felt were Old Testament provisions (Matthew 12:1, 2). In all, there were 613 laws, 248 positive, 365 negative, which they felt were contained in the Torah, or the Law of Moses. Their next task was to erect a hedge around the Law so that they would not be guilty of breaking God's law by ignorance or accident. For the Sabbath, for example, the Pharisees extracted a code of 39 prohibitions from the Law of Moses. To these they added 31 oral customs, which they were so convinced were correct interpretation of the Mosaic code that they claimed these "traditions of the elders" to have come from Moses (Mark 7:3).

It is commendable that the Pharisees had a desire to be righteous, and that they had such a reverence for the revelation of God that they would go to great lengths to avoid breaking His commandments. The tragedy of the Pharisees, however, lay in their self-righteousness, which we are reminded is as filthy rags (Isaiah 64:6). Theirs was a yoke that no man could bear (Matthew 23:4). In their zealous round of precept-keeping, they were blinded to the pride and guilt in their own hearts. It was for their hypocrisy and religious pride that Jesus chastised them. Their blind zeal eventually led them to seek to kill Jesus. However, there were some who were good and sincere people, who truly longed for the righteousness of God. Nicodemus, who sought out Jesus by night, was a Pharisee. Simon invited Jesus to a banquet (Luke 7:37). Paul was a Pharisee before his conversion.

Although the entire caste of the Pharisees can be viewed as an extremist group within Judaism, it was not just a simple solid bloc. There were two main schools of rabbinical interpretation that furnished the principal division within Pharisaism. The School of Shammai was known for rigoristic interpretation—a demand for precision and rigidity. He was a *fundamentalist*. It is interesting that Shammai came from a rich, aristocratic family. The opposing school of legal interpretation was led by Hillel, who gave a greater latitude to the interpretation of the law. Hillel was closer to the common people, and understood that if the Law was interpreted too rigorously only the rich could afford to bear the consequences. Gamaliel, the son of Hillel, demonstrated considerable moderation in his dealing with the Christians in Jerusalem (Acts 5:33–40). Although there was a breach between the common people and the religious parties, Pharisaism did have more attraction for the lower middle and artisan classes than did the Sadducees.

The Sadducees

The name "Sadducees" probably goes back to the high priest in the time of King David, Zadok. The family of Zadok held the high priesthood until the turbulent times of the Maccabean revolt. During the period of Seleucid control of Palestine, the Sadducean high priests were the chief negotiators with foreign governments. This gave considerable political power to them. With the increase in political power, there was a corresponding decrease in spiritual fervor. The author of the apocryphal 1 Maccabees regarded them as traitors to the tradition of their fathers (1 Maccabees 1:15).

During the reign of the Herods in Judea, the Sadducees did not fare well, but with the coming of the Roman procurators, during the lifetime of Jesus, the Sadducees regained their political power, controlling the high priesthood and the Sanhedrin. They numbered fewer than the Pharisees, but had considerable influence.

The Sadducees in Jesus' day were the sophisticated, urban class, most of whom lived in Jerusalem. They were educated and had wealth. This was the apex of the Jewish aristocracy. There was virtually no following among the masses.

There were important differences in belief between the Sadducees and the Pharisees. For one thing, the Sadducees accepted only the Law of Moses as the codebook for behavior, rejecting all the oral tradition which the Pharisees regarded with such reverence. Doctrinally, the Sadducees were "liberals." They rejected the existence of angels and spirits and denied the idea of a resurrection (Acts 23:8). The Pharisees at least were supernaturalists; the Sadducees were naturalists. Theirs was a rational religion more preoccupied with matters of current expedient interest than in eternal truths. They were more prone to compromise with Greek or Roman paganism for this reason. This willingness to negotiate with an alien world won them the enmity of ardent nationalists and zealous Jews. Caiaphas, the high priest, evidently was sensitive to their lack of popularity and the relative insecurity this occasioned (John 11:48).

A lesson of history may be learned from the Sadducees. With the destruction of the Temple in A.D. 70 the Sadducee party disappeared. A compromising, temporizing spirit was unable to withstand the shock of political revolution. The disbanding of the priesthood and the slaughter of the aristocracy in the terrible war spelled their doom. The religion of these sophisticated few did not have depth enough to endure crisis.

The Herodians

Various theories have been propounded to account for the origin of the Herodians and to outline their views. Some have questioned whether they were ever really a religious or political party at all. Possibly they represented an attitude and an outlook, primarily of influential Jews who supported the Herodian dynasty. This allegiance to Herod was a vote for Rome, since the Herods owed their existence to Roman power. Such an attitude was quite unpopular with the mass of the people who considered attachment to the Roman system, an invading foreign power, to be unpatriotic. Quite likely very few of the total population were outspoken Herodians.

The Herodians are referred to on two occasions in the Gospel narratives, in each case identified as enemies of Jesus. The first encounter was in Galilee (Mark 3:6); the second in Jerusalem (Mark 12:13; Matthew 22:16). On both occasions the Herodians are pictured as taking counsel with the Pharisees against Jesus. The striking feature of this is that the two groups, Pharisees and Herodians, really had little in common. In fact, their sympathies naturally lay in opposing directions. Their hatred of Jesus, however, was so great that they were willing to let personal differences drop in their common struggle against Jesus, whose life and message challenged their way of life and convicted them painfully.

It is interesting to look in on the Jerusalem encounter between the Herodians and Jesus. There the question of paying tribute to Caesar arose. The issue was really cast in such a way that they hoped to trap Jesus by whatever answer He gave. If He committed Himself as favoring paying taxes, they could accuse Him of submission to the foreign yoke. If He sided with the group that resented paying taxes to a foreign government, they could criticize His nationalism as an affront to Rome. Notice how skillfully Jesus eluded their cunning trap (Mark 12:17; Matthew 22:21).

The Zealots

One of the twelve apostles is called Simon the Zealot (Luke 6:15; Acts 1:13), possibly because of his temperament, but more likely because of his association with the fiery nationalist party, known as the Zealots. Paul refers to himself as being a religious zealot (Acts 22:3; Galatians 1:14), but it is doubtful whether this indicates more than an attitude of passionate concern. In fact, many members of the Jerusalem church were described as "zealots for the law" (Acts 21:20).

Who were the political zealots of Jesus' day? Josephus, the historian, describes the party of the Zealots as "the fourth philosophy" of Judaism. The first three were the Pharisees, the Sadducees, and the Essenes, of whom we shall have more to say in the next chapter. The Zealots appear to have been founded by one called Judas the Galilean, who led a revolt against Rome in A.D. 6 at the time that Quirinius governor of Syria, established a census for the purpose of collecting taxes (Acts 5:37). This was about ten years after the first census in which Mary and Joseph were required to go to the native home of Joseph to be enrolled (Luke 2:2). The Zealots led by Judas (not Iscariot) opposed the payment of tribute by Israel to a foreign power, particularly to a pagan emperor. They reasoned that this was treason to God, the only real king the Jews acknowledged. They sought to follow the tradition of Mattathias and the Maccabee heroes of their illustrious past who resisted the Seleucid attempt to paganize their land. Their zeal for the Law and for their nation was not crushed when the Romans wiped out Judas and his followers in the abortive revolt of A.D. 6. Members of Judas' family continued as Zealot leaders. Two of his sons were crucified by the procurator of Judea, Alexander, in A.D. 46. A third son, Menahem, attempted to seize control of the revolution against Rome which erupted in A.D. 66. It is quite likely that the underground agitation of the Zealots did much to foment the outbreak of that disastrous war which ended with the destruction of the Jewish nation in A.D. 70. The New Testament later epistles particularly 2 Peter, Jude and Hebrews, were written in that turbulent decade immediately prior to the fall of the Temple. Zealot pressure had made life miserable for Jewish Christians, for they cast the finger of suspicion on any of their people whose religious outlook was not identical with traditional Judaism.

Some think of the Zealots as the extreme right wing of the Pharisees, standing far removed from the negotiating spirit of the Sadducees. An example of this fanatical, uncompromising enmity to what they considered to be a dilution of their religious tradition is the episode recounted in Acts 23:12. Following Paul's arrest, a band of Jews vowed that they would not eat or drink until they had killed Paul. This seems to fit the description of a terrorist cloak-and-dagger attitude prevailing throughout the first century among the extremist Jews. These fanatical Jews would kill anyone if they thought that such a murder would aid their cause, hence they earned the dark name, *Assassins.*

The last stronghold of the Zealots was the fortress of Masada, not far from the Dead Sea. There the last 960 held out against a lengthy Roman siege. In May, A.D. 73, resigned to their fate, these fanatical loyalists committed mass suicide, a few survivors remaining to recount the tale of their bravery. Today it is the custom in modern Israel for all military recruits to make a pilgrimage to Masada, there to repeat the solemn words that symbolize the determination of the modern Israelis, "Masada shall not fall again."

Summary

Of the million-and-a-half to two million inhabitants of Palestine in Jesus' day, perhaps a third were Jews. The Jews were most heavily concentrated in the southern province of Judea, perhaps even being outnumbered by Greek-speaking Gentiles in the outlying northern province of Galilee. It is a tragic fact of history that Jesus came unto His own, and His own received Him not (John 1:11), for it was in the least-Jewish province that Jesus had His greatest welcome, and it was in Judea, the stronghold of Judaism, that He was so bitterly attacked from all quarters of Jewish society. How sad that the divisions within Judaism—Pharisee and Sadducee, Zealot and Herodian—closed ranks in their determination to be rid of the One who had come to die for them! Of all the organized and semi-organized parties of Judaism, none was sympathetic to Jesus. Only the poor of the land, the Amha-arets, heard Him with joy.

But, the message of the gospel is to "whosoever will." How wonderful that in that little band of Jesus' disciples there was Matthew, a toll-collector for the Romans, possibly a Herodian. And there was Simon the Zealot, too! From every party, from every background, Jesus still accepts those who will lay aside their own selfish, personal interests and surrender to the claims of the King of kings and Lord of lords!

4

Palestinian Judaism: The Dead Sea Community

According to the Jewish historian Josephus the three particularly important groups within first-century Judaism were the Pharisees, the Sadducees, and the Essenes. The New Testament makes abundant reference to the Pharisees and the Sadducees, but there is no direct reference at all to the Essenes. The reason for this is that the Essenes, unlike the other religious groups, lived apart from organized society in Palestine, preferring the seclusion of the Judean wilderness to the hustle and activity of the towns and villages. While the Pharisees and Sadducees were prominent and active in the social fabric of the day, the Essenes were a withdrawn people, living a kind of monastic existence, largely hidden from the public view, and quite mysterious until very recent years. The brief notices in Josephus, Philo of Alexandria, the Roman historian Pliny the Elder, and Hippolytus have provided us with the barest of information from ancient days regarding these unusual people.

An Exciting Discovery

In the spring of 1947 two Bedouin shepherd boys were grazing their sheep and goats at the edge of the northwest shore of the Dead Sea. It was the annual custom of the local Arab tribesmen to take advantage of the spring rains which turned the desolate wilderness green for a short time. There, at the mouth of a wadi, or deep gorge, that cut back into the towering, jagged cliffs along the shore, was the spring of Ein Feshkah. As the story is told, one of the animals strayed from the flocks. While wandering about among the cliffs just to the north of the spring, not far from the promontory on which were located the ancient ruins of Qumran, one of the shepherds, Muhammed ed-Dib, threw a rock into a small, round opening in the face of the cliff. Instead of hearing the sound he expected, the shepherd boy heard the shattering of pottery, and fled in fear. Later summoning their courage, the two boys returned to investigate, hoping perhaps to find buried treasure. It was not gold they found, but a treasure nonetheless. In the floor of the cave they found several large jars containing numerous decaying leather rolls. Little did they know that they had accidentally stumbled on documents two thousand years old, documents that the great dean of archaeologists, William F. Albright, was to pronounce as the greatest manuscript discovery of modern times.

Disappointed at their find, they did gather a few of the rolls. Eventually they sold some of them for about ten dollars to a shoemaker in Bethlehem, a town about twelve miles distant. The shoemaker sent a piece of one of the scrolls to an antiquities dealer in Jerusalem. The dealer showed the scrap to the late E. L. Sukenik, noted Jewish archaeologist of the Hebrew University in Jerusalem. Sukenik years before had studied in Chicago with W. F. Albright, and had learned the peculiarities of the Hebrew alphabet used during the time of Jesus. As soon as he saw the scrap of leather, he sensed that an important discovery had been made.

Arab-Israeli tension in late 1947 had reached the level of virtual war, with the partition of Palestine and the institution of the modern state of Israel only months away. Sukenik risked his life to enter the village of Bethlehem, located in Arab territory, to see the cobbler and his scrolls. In the midst of all the high drama of a thrilling spy novel, Sukenik managed to purchase three of the scrolls.

The cobbler had sold four of the scrolls to his Syrian archbishop, who in turn eventually brought them to America, hoping to sell them. These scrolls in time came into the possession of the son of Sukenik, Yigael Yadin, and the Hebrew University.

In the course of the next months and years, news of the value of the find led Arab Bedouins and trained archaeologists to vie with one another for further similar finds. The Arab-Israeli War of 1947-48 hampered activity, but in the years since, ten additional caves have been found in the general vicinity of the first one, and literally thousands of fragments of ancient manuscripts, together with several complete scrolls, have been located.

At first there was uncertainty about the connection between the cave documents and the abandoned ruins at Khirbet Qumran, but an excavation was undertaken at the site of the ruins by two prominent archaeologists, G. Lankester Harding, Director of Antiquities in Jerusalem, and R. P. Roland de Vaux, Director of the Ecole Biblique et Archéologique Francaise in Jerusalem. Five campaigns of digging were undertaken by this team between 1951 and 1956. This scientific exploration yielded a wealth of information, not only linking the scrolls to the ruins, but aiding in piecing together the history of that obscure people, the Essenes.

The Story of the Essenes

The archaeological *digs* at Qumran disclosed this site to be the center of a communal settlement dating from Hellenistic and Roman times, stretching two miles to the north of Qumran, and two miles south, along the cliffs. Apparently the people who resided there lived in caves, tents, and some masonry structures, but shared a number of aspects of life as common property. Their pottery was made in the same kiln, they read the same scrolls which appeared to come from a centrally located scriptorium, or writing room, and the entire monastic community shared an irrigation system. A central storehouse for both food and water has been located. All this points strongly in the direction of Qumran having been the center of the mysterious Essenes, for these artifacts tend to support the description of the Essenes given by Josephus.

The archaeological evidence permits a reconstruction of the

history of Qumran. Apparently there were three quite distinct periods, bounded by two destructions. The dating of these periods of occupation has been illuminated by the finding of coins, pottery, and other artifacts which had lain undisturbed for millennia in the various strata, or levels, at Qumran.

The first Essene settlement appears to have been built on the ruined foundations of a Judean fortress that had been destroyed about the sixth century B.C. More than one hundred coins located in the first level indicate that the first Essene occupation of the site occurred about 100 B.C., or shortly before. This places it in the Hasmonean period, and fits well the picture of the times. Evidently the corrupted priesthood was so distasteful to some of the Jews of that period that they formed a separate society, aloof from the Jerusalem priesthood altogether. Evidence from the site indicates that this first phase of occupation flourished until Herodian times, shortly before the birth of Christ. An earthquake in 31 B.C., during the reign of Herod the Great, destroyed the site. Josephus indicates that 30,000 Judeans died in that disaster.

The site was not immediately rebuilt. A generation later, during the time that Christ was a child and in the reign of Archelaus in Judea, a partial rebuilding of the site took place. This has been determined from the dating of coins found in the second level. The rebuilding did not alter the basic design of the foundations, and apparently the functions of the buildings were not changed, suggesting that the same group of people had returned. This second occupation appears to have endured without hindrance throughout the life of Christ and up to the time of the great Jewish uprising against Rome in A.D. 66. The blackened ruins and Roman arrowheads are mute evidence of the disaster that befell the monastic community of Qumran. The Roman general Vespasian dispatched a contingent of troops, the Tenth Legion, into the region of Jericho and the Dead Sea in the spring of A.D. 68, according to Josephus. Confirmation by the coins found at Qumran substantiate the story of Josephus, leading us to conclude that the end of the Essene community came at that time. Evidently disaster was swift, for the people did not have time to carry away their scrolls, which they had placed in nearby caves. The suddenness of the Roman assault is without doubt the reason that the scrolls were left unnoticed. The extremely dry climate in the region of the Dead Sea seems to account for their remarkable preservation through the long centuries, and the difficult terrain guaranteed their inaccessibility.

The third period of occupation followed hard upon the end of the Essene period. Evidently Qumran became an outpost of the Roman garrison located in Jericho, with their assignment being to stand guard against possible guerrilla forays from the southern Judean wilderness. Evidences of temporary, barracks living indicate that this phase of occupation was rather brief. Apparently the Roman soldiers abandoned the site before the end of the first century. For all practical purposes, this was the end of the Qumran occupation, until archaeologists of the twentieth century moved to the site. Thus, the Essene community and the Dead Sea Scrolls can be dated between 100 B.C. and A.D. 100, spanning the New Testament age and the times of Christ.

Khirbet Qumran

Excavation of the two Essene levels at Khirbet ("ruins") Qumran indicates that basically the same pattern of living prevailed throughout their existence. The main communal center was a walled fortress, well-situated on the plateau at the edge of Wadi Qumran, whose precipitous sides made it fairly easy to defend from that direction. The unprotected sides were safeguarded by walls, atop which was a tower for the use of a sentry. Although the Essenes were not a militant people, the isolation of the community in the rugged wilderness made defense against lawless marauding bands a necessity. Surrounding the main center were the community agricultural enterprises, and some outlying habitations.

A striking feature of the entire complex is the ingenious aqueduct and water storage capacity they engineered. Some of the baths or pools found in the settlement may have had religious significance, for ceremonial washing was an important feature of their worship. However, it does appear that the main purpose of the elaborate water system was to provide for the long dry season of that most inhospitable region. Josephus indicates that there were 4,000 Essenes, some of whom were scattered in the towns and villages of Judea, but most of them lived in the wilderness, and according to Pliny, they lived on the northwest shore of the Dead Sea, precisely where Qumran is located. It would take considerable effort to provide water for a sizable community in desert country. To be sure, the Essenes were a remarkable people.

In the main building were several interesting rooms. One large room, equipped with tables and ink pots (some dried ink still remained after all this time!), quite obviously was the scriptorium or writing room, where many, if not all, of the Dead Sea Scrolls were prepared. This was quite likely the area where the scrolls were normally kept. Evidently their hasty removal to the caves nearby was an emergency measure occasioned by the threat of Roman conquest.

The main building contained a large assembly room, complete with a platform at one end for the use of the reader or leader of the meetings. Adjacent to this room were found evidences of cookware, indicating that a common meal was eaten in the assembly room, a feature of their worship.

Elsewhere in the complex of structures at Qumran are vestiges of a pottery, a bakery, a gram mill, a tannery, and curiously, an elaborate cemetery.

The Essenes' burial customs disclose something of their belief and practice. The bones of the animals eaten in their sacred common meal were carefully preserved and buried in jars within the compound. Outside the main area was their own burial ground. Evidently the central burial site was for men only. Interestingly, women and children were buried nearby, indicating that the colony was not entirely celibate. Some think that originally the monastic community was strictly for men, but through the years it became a mixed community. Some think that although it was primarily celibate, they did have provision for married people and families to live nearby and participate with the main celibate group, as a sort of second order.

Examination of the scrolls in conjunction with the excavations at Khirbet Qumran reveals previously hidden facts about the daily life and belief of the ancient Essenes. Before we conclude our visit with this fascinating group of people, let us look briefly at some of their peculiar views, and then determine the significance of these people for our understanding of Bible times.

Essenism

Among the Dead Sea Scrolls are manuscripts that provide a revealing insight into the beliefs that energized the Qumran community. Most significant of these are "The Manual of Discipline," "The War of the Sons of Light and the Sons of Darkness," "The Thanksgiving Psalms," the "Commentary on Habakkuk," and "The Damascus Document." From these manuscripts it appears that the sect of the Essenes was founded during the Hasmonean dynasty by a "Teacher of Righteousness." This leader repudiated the official priesthood in Jerusalem and established a completely self-contained community in the wilderness, there to prepare for the coming of the Messiah. They developed a closely-knit organization, with the entire community subject to a priest-president of a counsel of elders, twelve in number. The council was composed of both lay people and priests. Under their discipline the entire community lived and worked, having all property in common and each performing a specified task for the benefit of the entire congregation.

The Essenes considered themselves to be a special group who bent every energy toward preparing for the coming of the Messiah. They were an "army of the Lord," who engaged in all manner of disciplinary activity and rites of purification so as to be ready for the imminent coming of the Messiah. Theirs was a rigorous life, far more ascetic than that of the Pharisees.

Utterly devoted to the keeping of the Law, they devoted much of their time to study, meditation, and ritual centering in the books of Moses. To speak ill of Moses or his revelation was deserving of the severest punishment. The Sabbath was safeguarded by a prescribed code of conduct that made Pharisaism look quite tame indeed!

Those wishing to join the Essenes went through a period of initiation lasting a total of two years. Even in the first year the novice was allowed to wear the white garments that the entire community habitually wore. At the end of the first year, he underwent a ritual cleansing in water, a kind of baptism ceremony. An additional year was required, however, before he could be admitted to the sacred meal which the full-fledged members ate together. Admission to this rank was accompanied by the swearing of various solemn oaths.

A typical day in Qumran began before sunrise with morning prayers, facing the sun. The morning was occupied with work, under the supervision of appointed overseers. At noon the members bathed and ate a meal together. The afternoon was occupied with resumption of their work detail. In the evening another common meal was shared.

An interesting feature of the customs of the Essenes was the repetition of baptism at frequent intervals. The elders of the group repeatedly examined the younger members to insure the purity of the fellowship. So rigid was their routine that any who broke the regulations of the community were severely penalized, usually by banishment from the colony. How little they knew of grace! Theirs was a system of works-righteousness that Paul reminds us is doomed to failure (Romans 3:21–30). Jesus came to give men a new heart, a heart from which good works could flow. The Essenes, much like their cousins the Pharisees, were intent on earning a place in the kingdom of God by the earnest keeping of rules. How dreary their round of endless purification rites must have been!

The Essene community was established originally by priests who revolted from the apostasy they detected in Jerusalem. With them came the concept of sacrifice. They objected to the

Temple sacrifices in Jerusalem, considering them to be polluted. At Qumran the priests instituted a system of sacrifice,
to which the burial jars of animal bones testify. Again, one
observes that not far from Qumran, just outside Jerusalem the
true sacrifice, the Lamb of God which taketh away the sin of
the world, died. The Essenes somehow in their blind zeal missed
that to which all the Old Testament sacrifices pointed!

An important theme that runs through Essene literature is
their sense of expectancy regarding the coming of the Messiah.
This current of feeling was evident in other aspects of Judaism
at the time of the coming of Christ, too, but in Essenism it was
more predominant. They identified the coming Messiah as "The
Teacher of Righteousness," who would be a Zadokite priest,
and who would be responsible for bringing a national and earthly
deliverance to the Jews. How like the disciples at the time of
the ascension of Christ who still did not quite understand that
the first coming of Christ was not to be marked by an earthly
reign (Acts 1:6). Some think that the Essenes were actually
looking for two Messiahs, one to be the priestly teacher, the
other to be the military conqueror. In any event, their mater-
ialized conception of the Messiah seemed to blind them, along
with much of the rest of Judaism, to the King who came into
their midst as a babe.

The Significance of the Essenes

Uncovering of the materials of Qumran has had special importance for the conservative Bible scholar. In the documents
of the Dead Sea community are quotations from all the Old
Testament books, with the exception of Esther. Previously the
oldest Old Testament manuscripts available were no earlier
than about A.D. 900. With the Qumran find, the scholar has
been able in one giant step to push back toward the original
writings one thousand years! The similarity between the quotations of the Old Testament found at Qumran and what we
have previously used as the basis of our modern translations
gives considerable support to the amazing accuracy with which

God's revelation to the Old Testament prophets and writers has been transmitted to our day. The literature of the Essenes has been a means of underscoring the providential care of our heavenly Father over His wonderful Word, the Bible!

Although the Essenes lived apart from society of the first century, there has been an indirect value for the New Testament Bible scholar from the findings at Qumran. Critical scholars of a previous generation seemed to delight in arguing that some of the Pauline epistles, and books like the Gospel of John, were really not apostolic at all—they belonged to the second century! One of the reasons set forward by such liberal critics was that portions of the New Testament seemed to reflect ideas felt to be too late for the first century. For example, Paul in Colossians and John in the Gospel and in his first epistle, seem to be aware of a danger threatening the Church, an idea called Gnosticism. This threat was known to have been a serious problem to the Church of the second century but little information was available until recent years to indicate Gnosticism to have been a prominent idea earlier, particularly in Palestine. Now, however, owing to various finds, and confirmed by the Qumran materials, a rather well-developed form of Gnosticism seems to have been part of Near Eastern culture much earlier than had previously been supposed. One direct impact of this has been the dramatic shift in attitude by great scholars like W. F. Albright regarding the dating of the Gospel of John. Albright, who used to hold John to be a second-century document, now concedes that it belongs to the first century, and may even be the earliest of the Gospels!

With the discovery of the Dead Sea Scrolls, the greatest excitement erupted over possible connections between the Essene community and the early Christian Church, or at least with figures like John the Baptist. John the Baptist, for instance, was known to have frequented the Jordan wilderness, which was, of course, in the area of Qumran. Was he, then, perhaps an Essene? Was Jesus and His message an outgrowth of Essenism? After the initial hysteria had subsided, it became apparent that the superficial similarities between the Essenes on the one hand, and John the Baptist and Jesus on the other were far outweighed by fundamental differences. It is evident that there was no direct connection at all.

The Qumran community were archlegalists, seeking salvation by the keeping of the Mosaic Law. Jesus came to provide a better covenant, not based on works, but on faith in His atonement. The Qumran people knew nothing of an atonement by their expected Messiah; they had no sense that their "Teacher of Righteousness" would fulfill the types and symbols of Old Testament sacrifice in himself. The Essenes were forever going through purification rituals, washings, and baptisms. How different is the message of the Book of Hebrews. The work of Christ at Calvary was efficacious once for all (Hebrews 9:28). The Christian testimony of baptism needs no repetition (Hebrews 6:1–3). The Qumran people were preoccupied with a coming earthly Messiah; the Christians looked backward with confidence to the redemption wrought by Christ, as well as to the future day when He shall come as King of kings! And, how different is the exclusivist attitude of the Qumran community. They hated all who did not belong to their little band, considering themselves alone as the elect of God. Jesus came in compassion and concern to die for all men, so that whosoever will may come!

Summary

Although the New Testament makes no direct reference to the Essenes, they do form a significant part of the Palestinian world in the times of Jesus. For the Bible scholar, some awareness of who they were and what they were like will help to complete his picture of life in Palestine. Because of the spectacular nature of the discovery of the Dead Sea Scrolls, some sincere students of God's Word have been unsettled by rash and misleading statements regarding the connection between the Essenes and the Early Church. It is important to know that, although the Essene story is interesting for background information, there is no direct link between them and the beginnings of the Church.

5

Palestinian Judaism: Temple and Synagogue

If you lived in Jerusalem in the times of Jesus you could not fail to notice an impressive building, the great Temple. Together with its cloisters and courtyards, it dominated the highest spot in this hilly city. Just as its gilded pinnacles and gleaming marble columns commanded the awe of arriving pilgrims, so did the Temple and its services dominate the religious life of first century Palestine. If the Temple was the center of national religious life, the synagogue was its local counterpart, deeply influencing the life of the town, village, and neighborhood. Temple priests and scribes of the Law were the influential people in that very religious society into which Jesus came.

The Temple and Its Activity

The Temple of Solomon, built in the tenth century B.C. (1 Kings 6:1), had been destroyed in 586 B.C. at the time of the Babylonian Captivity, as we have seen. Upon the return from Captivity, Zerubbabel led in the erection of a second Temple, which was completed only after considerable delay. Never considered as impressive as the first Temple, the second suffered the ravages of pillage by Seleucids and Romans. Eventually, Herod the Great, to curry favor with the Jews, launched an impressive restoration project that was not finally completed until just prior to the terrible destruction of A.D. 70.

Herod's Temple was dazzling in its grandeur. The entire complex stood in a great walled enclosure covering about twenty-six acres in the eastern portion of the city, overlooking the

Kidron Valley. Across the valley to the east lay the Garden of Gethsemane, a frequent resting place for Jesus and His disciples. One can easily imagine Jesus in the Garden, brooding over the scene spread before Him, sighing "How often would I have gathered thy children together, even as a hen gathereth her chickens under her wings, and ye would not" (Matthew 23:37). The splendor of the Temple ritual and furnishings masked the emptiness of the religion of the people, for in the midst of all the pageantry and pomp of official religion, Jesus was shut out of their lives.

Within the outer walls was a spacious area open to the general public. Stalls for money changers and other shopkeepers made this busy area, known as the "Court of the Gentiles," a veritable marketplace (John 2:14). In the northwest corner of the enclosure was the Castle of Antonia, the Roman military headquarters in Jerusalem for the use of the governors at the times of religious festivals. With thousands of pilgrims thronging the city at high religious celebrations, during the earthly life of Jesus it was the regular practice of the governors to abide temporarily in the Temple area to keep order and to prevent a possible uprising. The priests' robes were kept in the Roman fortress, a symbol of the subjection of the Jews to Rome.

Within the outer court was an inner courtyard, slightly raised, and set off from the outer court by a low wall with numerous gates. These gates were carefully guarded by a detachment of Jewish Temple police given special authority by the Romans. No Gentiles were permitted beyond the outer court into this special area. In 1935 an inscription was discovered which apparently had been part of the inner wall. It reads:

> No non-Jew is permitted to pass beyond this boundary-
> point. Anyone who does, does so at his own risk, and will
> be liable to the death-penalty.[1]

Within this sanctuary, there were three divisions. The Court of the Women was entered first, possibly through the Gate Beautiful. Here were the chests for the gifts the people gave for the maintenance of the services (Mark 12:41–44). Farther in, there was another division, somewhat raised, called the

Court of Israel, from which the women were excluded. Just beyond, surrounding the Temple and the altar itself, was the Court of the Priests.

The Temple itself, built of massive marble blocks, and adorned with gold, must have been an impressive sight. Immediately in front of the entrance, in the Court of the Priests, stood the great altar of burnt offering. Near it was the place where the sacrificial animals were prepared for offering. Close by was the laver used by the priests for ceremonial washing. Entering the Temple one first came to a porch, or vestibule area, and then immediately into a large room known as the Holy Place which contained the table of shewbread, the altar of incense, and a seven-branched candlestick. Behind this room was the cubicle known as the Holy of Holies, separated from the Holy Place by a thick curtain or veil (Matthew 27:51). Only the priests were allowed to enter the Holy Place. And once a year on the Day of Atonement the High Priest entered the inner sanctuary, the Holy of Holies, to make propitiation there for the sins of the people. Striking by way of contrast with pagan temples of the first century was the fact that the Holy of Holies was empty. There was no image there which the people worshiped. In fact, sometime during the Exile the ark of the covenant had been lost, and even that was no longer present as it had been in Solomon's day. The God of the Jews was a Spirit, not a creature made with hands, such as the Gentiles worshiped.

Each morning at about 9 and each afternoon at about 3 the daily, or "continual," burnt offering was presented by the priests on behalf of the people. The priests alternated in the temple services by divisions, or *courses.* Those on duty in the regular rotation slept in the adjoining cloisters. Before daylight the priests who wished to be available for that day's ceremonies bathed and dressed and then gathered in a room for the drawing of lots. To avoid any feeling of favoritism, the number needed for that day's services were so chosen (Luke 1:8, 9). Additional lots determined which specific task each priest would be assigned, whether it be preparing the wood for the altar fire (which was never supposed to go out), the slaying of the sacrifice, removing the ashes, throwing the blood against the altar, or preparing the meal offering of flour, or the drink offering.

With the coming of daylight, the gates of the Temple were opened. The people thronged to the various areas to which they were permitted, the women remaining somewhat apart from the pilgrims who could enter the Court of Israel. Following a brief devotional period, the priests entered the temple with a censer of incense, while the people worshiping outside prayed silently (Luke 1:10). When the priests came out of the Holy Place they then threw the various parts of the sacrifice on the altar for burning. The pouring out of the drink offering was the signal for the choir of Levites to begin chanting (or singing) the psalm scheduled for that day's service. A variety of musical instruments accompanied this part of the service (Psalm 150:3–5). Periodically two priests blew on silver trumpets, each time the people prostrating themselves before the Lord. When the main sacrifice was concluded, private sacrifices were offered, each Jew bringing the animal for offering at his own expense. One common sacrifice was the Mosaic requirement for cleansing forty days after the birth of a child (Lev. 12:6–8). Either a lamb or a dove was acceptable depending on their economic circumstances (Luke 2:22–24). Mary and Joseph brought a dove, evidence of their poverty. The afternoon service was substantially the same as the morning service, with the exception that the seven-branched golden lampstand was lighted for this service.

The Great Festivals

In addition to the daily sacrifices in the Temple, there were five great annual feasts, or festivals, that punctuated the religious calendar. Because the Jewish year consisted of twelve lunar months, periodically it was necessary to add an extra month to keep the year approximately equivalent to the solar year, such as we use. For this reason it is possible only to approximate the dating of the feasts by our calendar.

The Jewish religious year began with the great Passover

feast, occurring about April by our calendar. This was by far the most important of the feasts, and attracted large numbers of visitors to Jerusalem. It was the custom of Mary and Joseph to make this annual pilgrimage to Jerusalem. On such an occasion when Jesus was twelve years old, He became separated from His parents in the crowd, very likely in one of the booths in the Court of the Gentiles where the rabbis held informal discussion sessions (Luke 2:40–51). Jesus appeared at the Passover during His public ministry, likely in four successive years, according to the chronology of His ministry sketched by the gospel writers (John 2:13; 5:1; 6:4; and 12:1).

About the middle of the month preceding the Passover, workmen busied themselves repairing bridges and roads, preparing for the flood of visitors expected to inundate the city. Even the tombs were whitewashed so visitors would not be "contaminated" by inadvertently touching them! Without doubt it was in reference to just such a marked tomb that Jesus said to the Pharisees, "Woe unto you . . . for ye are like unto whited sepulchres, which outwardly appear beautiful, but inwardly are full of dead men's bones" (Matthew 23:27). At home, diligent housecleaning and scouring of utensils occupied the people. On the day of the feast, every male Jew within a radius of fifteen miles of Jerusalem was expected to come to the city, bringing his lamb with him. Pilgrims from far and near joined the throng. The population of the city swelled to enormous proportions during this important feast time, which lasted for eight days, as many as 125,000 making the trip. Some estimate the number of pilgrims at over a million, although this seems to be an unbelievable burden for a city the size of Jerusalem.

At the Temple, a large number of priests were on duty to process the lamb sacrifices. Each animal was slain, its blood poured out at the altar, where a drain carried the blood quickly away. The animal was skinned, and quickly dressed. The fat was burned at the Temple, but the rest of the lamb was taken home, where the Passover meal was eaten by the family, in accordance with the instructions supplied in Exodus 12. How wonderful it is that Jesus became our Passover Lamb, so that we need no longer depend on the blood of animals! Once and for all, the great price for our sin was paid (Hebrews 10:8–14).

The next important festival of the religious year occurred fifty days after the close of the Passover week. This was called The Feast of Weeks, or Pentecost (meaning fifty). Jewish tradition indicates that this feast, occurring in June of our year, commemorates the giving of the Law at Sinai to Moses. It was characterized by the offering of two wave loaves of leavened bread, made from the freshly harvested grain. This feast attracted many pilgrims to Jerusalem (Acts 2:5). It represented a thanksgiving for the early harvest. It is significant that the Holy Spirit was poured out on the disciples at the time of the firstfruits (Acts 2). This Jewish feast became the birthday of the Church. Has not God who poured out the Holy Spirit at the time of the firstfruits promised also to pour out His Spirit at the time of the latter-rain? Surely we have been seeing a bountiful harvest in these last days.

About the first of October the Jewish civil year began with the Feast of Trumpets, now called "Rosh Hashana." It was a time of horn-blowing and merry-making all day long in the Temple. Not many pilgrims made their way to Jerusalem for this festive occasion, for it was customary to observe this New Year's celebration in the local synagogues, as well as in the Jerusalem Temple.

About a week after the Feast of Trumpets the great Day of Atonement was observed. The important feature of this solemn occasion was the presentation of the annual atonement by the high priest. Just once in the year the high priest ventured into the Holy of Holies. Dressed in a simple white linen garment, carrying a censer of coals from the altar, and with a bowl of blood from a freshly killed bullock that had been offered as a sin-offering, the high priest ventured within the veiled sanctuary to sprinkle the blood on the mercy seat. A goat was slain and its blood was also sprinkled on the mercy seat, on the altar of incense in the Holy Place, and the altar of burnt sacrifice just outside the Temple door. The high priest placed his hands upon the head of a second goat, confessing the sins of the people.

The goat was then led out into the wilderness and set free, evidently to symbolize the carrying away of the sins of the people (Leviticus 16:11–22). How wonderfully Christ fulfilled the typology of the Day of Atonement, making propitiation for our sins at Calvary, so that we need neither priest nor bullock to make a way to God for us (Hebrews 9:6–12).

Within a week after the Day of Atonement, usually about the middle of October, was the Feast of Tabernacles. This feast lasted eight days and was designed to commemorate the wandering in the wilderness. It served as a time of thanksgiving at the end of the fall harvest season. An interesting feature of this observance was the construction of temporary huts made of branches, symbolizing the temporary nature of the wilderness experience. Special sacrifices were offered during the course of the week, but the high point of the celebration came on the eighth day, a time of great celebration marking the end of the Jewish religious year. At a climactic moment on the last day of the festival was the pouring out of water from a golden pitcher at the altar of burnt offering, in full view of the crowd and likely at a breathless moment in which the crowd was hushed and quiet. Immediately following this ceremony was the singing of the great Hallel (Psalms 113–118) and the lighting of four great candlesticks. At precisely the dramatic moment, Jesus broke the silence with His electric declaration, "If any man thirst, let him come unto me and drink. He that believeth on me, as the scripture hath said, from within him shall flow rivers of living water" (John 7:37–39). This He spoke prophetically of the outpouring of the Holy Spirit. And, how like a river of living water is the mighty baptism of the Holy Spirit. All who thirst, let them come and drink.

Two additional feasts celebrated by Jewry since the time of the Maccabees have been the Feast of Lights and the Feast of Purim. The Feast of Lights, or "Hanukkah," is celebrated about the time of the Christian Christmas. This feast, although not properly part of the Jewish prescribed religious calendar since it did not come from the Mosaic legislation, nonetheless was most likely a feature of family life in Jesus' home. It was a happy occasion commemorating the cleansing of the Temple in 164 B.C. The Jewish homes were gaily lighted and the children were told again the heroic stories of the Maccabees. This was a family occasion, rather than a Temple ceremony.

In March the Feast of Purim commemorates the salvation of the Jews from destruction through the courage of Esther. This special observation was centered in the synagogue rather than the temple itself. The entire Book of Esther was read in the synagogue. It was a time of national pride roughly corresponding to our Fourth of July. It is possible that John 5:1 refers to this occasion, but this is not certain.

Scribes and Rabbis

In the ancient Near East, scribes had served a useful purpose in secular society as public secretaries (Jeremiah 36:4). By the time of Jesus, however, the term "scribe" had taken on a distinctive meaning signifying a special religious function. Our first glimpse of this new role of the scribe comes at the time of the Exile in Babylon. The priests had become special custodians of the Mosaic law during the captivity, the most noted of whom was Ezra (Nehemiah 8:9). At first the office seems to have been strongly identified with the priesthood, but eventually a separate class of professional law-scholars emerged, not all of whom were priests. The Sanhedrin in the time of Jesus was composed of priests, respected laymen, and scribes (Matthew 16:21). Ezra 7:10 pictures vividly the basic functions of the scribe in that day: "For Ezra had set his heart to seek the law of Jehovah, and to do it, and to teach in Israel statutes and ordinances."

By New Testament days, great respect had attached to the scribes. Sometimes they were referred to as "teachers of the law," or simply "teachers." The term "master" was not uncommon. They were also known as "lawyers" (Luke 7:30), for as experts in the law of Moses their word was considered authoritative in matters both religious and civil. Their influence extended throughout the villages of Judea and Galilee (Luke 5:17).

Perhaps the most significant title given to the scribes in the time of Jesus was "rabbi," meaning literally "my great one." By the time of the New Testament this term of respectful address was commonly employed, not only in speaking to a scribe, but in referring to him, as well. This is the term that Nicodemus used in his conversation with Jesus (John 3:2), reflecting the esteem with which Nicodemus held Him.

The scribes, in spite of their respected position in the community, supported themselves with the work of their hands. Some rabbis were carpenters, others stone-masons, and some followed other crafts. Paul was a tentmaker (Acts 18:3). Most of the scribes in the time of Jesus were Pharisees, but not all were (Mark 2:16). The work of the scribes fell into three areas. First, they preserved the law. They studied the law and defended it. Theirs was the responsibility of making fresh applications to new problems in daily life as they emerged. Hence, they "added" to the law, producing a body of material which became known as "the tradition of the elders" (Matthew 15:2). Jesus frequently clashed with these men who were so scrupulous about details, while missing the basic need for a new heart and an inner change.

The scribes also had the task of teaching the law. In connection with the local synagogue, a kind of elementary school was established, presided over by scribes. There the children learned to read from the Hebrew Scriptures, to write, and to do simple arithmetic. More advanced theological education was provided by particularly famous scribes, who gathered about them followers, or disciples. These noted rabbis held discussions in a room of the synagogue or in one of the chambers situated in the outer court of the Temple. For the benefit of their students, these rabbis on occasion held formal disputations, or debates among themselves. In some respects, Jesus was like a typical Jewish scribe. He called disciples to follow Him. These followers addressed Him as "Rabbi" (John 1:38). However, Jesus differed strikingly from the scribes. He startled his hearers by the authority He commanded (Matthew 7:28). He did not appeal to the traditions heaped up by earlier scribes, but depended solely on the authority of the Hebrew Scriptures and Himself alone. The Word, both written and living, is the authority in which believers in all ages have safely put their whole trust.

The third area of activity of the scribe was judicial. In Judea local courts, composed of at least three judges, handled most of the civil and religious problems that emerged in the community. In cases punishable by death a court of at least twenty-three judges had to give the decision. In Jerusalem, the "supreme court" was the Sanhedrin, composed of 71 persons—the elders (the Jewish aristocracy), the high priest (and those who had previously so served), and the scribes. Under Pilate, in the time of Jesus, the Sanhedrin had considerable authority, but decisions requiring the death sentence had to be ratified by the governor. Jesus was tried before the Sanhedrin (Matthew 26:59). It is an irony of history that this august body, noted for its fairness and justice, should engage in what scholars have considered to be a shocking abuse of their own law, the mockery of honor in the cruel trial of Jesus. Perhaps it was divine judgment that caused the abolition of the Sanhedrin in A.D. 70 when Titus, the Roman general, swept into the city.

The Synagogue

As important an institution as the synagogue has been throughout Jewish history, it is strange that its origins are so obscure. In spite of this lack of definite information, scholars generally agree that the synagogue arose during the Babylonian Captivity. Quite likely, pious Jews far from their homes in Babylon first gathered together in homes on the Sabbath for prayer and the reading of their Scriptures. Upon their return from Captivity, special meetinghouses were erected, in addition to the Temple. By the time of Jesus, synagogues were to be found throughout Palestine, and beyond, in all cities of the Empire where there were at least ten adult male Jews. Jerusalem alone is said to have had as many as 480 synagogues. In the larger cities, some synagogues seem to have been composed of special national-interest groups (Acts 6:9).

Originally, the study of the Law and prayer took the place of the Temple sacrifices during the Captivity. However, the synagogue became so effective as a means of cementing the Jewish community together, providing an invaluable community center for religious instruction, that it was carefully maintained even after the restoration of the Temple sacrifices.

The local synagogue was often an elaborate building, situated on the highest spot in the village or town. Archaeological evidence indicates that the buildings were made to face toward Jerusalem, the site of the Temple. Inside the synagogue, there were several furnishings of significance. The chest, or "ark," which contained the Old Testament Scriptures, was at one end. Near the ark was a raised platform on which the Scripture reader and prayer leader stood. The most learned scribe was given a special seat, called "Moses' seat" (Matthew 23:2). Several rows of seats just in front of the platform, facing the congregation, were considered places of honor. These were the "best seats" which the Pharisees and the scribes sought to occupy (Matthew 23:6).

The local synagogue was supervised by a council of laymen, or elders. A scribe or rabbi was not in charge of the conduct of the services, but, rather, one of the local elders was appointed to serve as "a ruler of the synagogue" (Luke 8:41). His tasks included the maintenance of the building and the supervision of the Sabbath morning services. He selected the persons each week who were to read the Scripture lesson, and invited noted rabbis to give comments in the course of the service. The form of service generally included, in addition to various prayers, a regular reading from the Old Testament, in such fashion that the Scriptures were read through in about three and a half years. The Scripture passages were read in Hebrew, but following each reading, a translation into Aramaic, the language of the common people, was given. This Aramaic paraphrase was called a "Targum." When a scribe was present, an exposition on the Scripture for the day was invited from him. Jesus participated in this fashion in the synagogue at Nazareth, startling the people by announcing that the passage from Isaiah that had been read was being fulfilled in Him (Luke 4:21).

Summary

Jesus frequented the temple services and participated in the synagogues of His day. From the typology of Temple feasts and from the Scriptures read in the weekly synagogue meetings, He proclaimed that the Messiah had come. Although the Temple and its ritual gradually faded from significance as the Church became more and more Gentile in its composition, the synagogue furnished an invaluable point of contact throughout the Empire for the apostles to proclaim Christ. Even the general layout of the synagogue, in structure and in operation, became a useful pattern for the churches of the New Testament. Jesus employed every aspect of the religious life of the people that He could to get them to see that Salvation had come. That so few could see the Messiah in the midst of their zealous round of religious activity is a sad truth indeed. Yet, how many today may there be who have every bit as much succeeded in crowding Christ out of first place in their heart of hearts.

---

[1]A. C. Bouquet, *Everyday Life in New Testament Times* (New York: Charles Scribner's Sons, 1953), p. 199.

6

Daily Life in Palestine

When Jesus lived on earth He sought by every means possible to communicate His love to the people. He lived close to them, sharing their daily joys and woes. When He spoke to them of eternal issues, He skillfully clothed His language with illustrations drawn from their common experiences in the field and the village, at home and in the marketplace. He loved the people so much that He took infinite pains to make His message plain. Let us look in on the daily life of which our Lord so often spoke. As we do, it may be that some passage of Scripture will become freshly alive to you. Special acknowledgment is due Joseph Gift[1] and G. M. Mackie,[2] from whose excellent books much of the material in this chapter has been gleaned.

At Home

Home was the center of life for the Palestinian Jews. It was usually very humble, consisting of but one room, walled with clay, having a dirt floor. The more prosperous had homes built of kiln-dried brick. Only the very wealthy could afford limestone houses. Usually the flat roof was composed of layers of reeds cemented with lime, for waterproofing, with openings in the raised wall for water to run off. When there was more than one room in the dwelling, they were arranged so as to form a kind of courtyard in the center, with the doors opening onto the courtyard. Running around inside the courtyard was usually a narrow covered walkway to protect the family in time of inclement weather. It was probably this portion of the roof that was removed in the story of the healing of the man with palsy (Mark 2:4).

Because of the mild weather that favors Palestine, much of the actual living of the people was in the out-of-doors. Frequently the house had an outside staircase that led to the roof where much of the entertaining took place. In hot weather, it was customary to sleep on the roof. A portion of the roof was covered over to afford some protection from the intense rays of the sun. It was to such an "upper room" that Jesus and His disciples retired for the Last Supper (Mark 14:15), and that later His disciples awaited Pentecost (Acts 1:13). Nicodemus probably talked with Jesus under the starlit Judean sky on such a rooftop (John 3:1).

Inside the house, one might see plain walls coated with lime or, in the houses of the rich, ornately decorated wood, marble, and ivory mosaics. Windows were small, to prevent the entrance of robbers, and frequently covered with latticework, since window glass was unknown to them. The rooms were quite dark, therefore, and it was necessary to furnish them with a lamp, which was usually placed on a shelf in the center pole of the room which supported the roof. The lamp, being portable, was taken into the narrow streets at night to illumine the way. The villagers were well acquainted with the lamps of which Jesus spoke in the story of the wise and foolish virgins (Matthew 25:1–13).

The family slept on the floor on pallets; those resembled quilts, being pads stuffed with cotton or wool. The palsied man whom Jesus healed and asked to "take up his bed," had just such a pallet (Matthew 9:6). It was customary for the entire family to sleep in a row in the same room, hence, in the teaching on importunity in prayer, Jesus refers to the man who is with his children in bed (Luke 11:7). He could not arise without disturbing the entire family.

The common people ate simple fare. Baked wheat or barley cakes were a staple of their diet, and the process of preparing the meal and baking it was the principal domestic chore. The village mill was operated by the women, who usually ground together in pairs, since it was such arduous work (Matthew 24:41). The mill consisted of two heavy stones, one set on top of the other, the top one having a handle for turning it around on the same axis as the bottom stone. The reference to the millstone in Matthew 18:6 would symbolize for the people an exceedingly heavy weight. It was important in preparing the grain for grinding that it be carefully sifted, so that the darnel or tares would be removed. Poorly cultivated fields abounded with such unwanted growth (Matthew 13:7). How significant to the people of Jesus' day that He should pray for Peter that he be not cast out with the refuse (Luke 22:31). In that culture in which bread was the basis of diet, no one could miss the significance of Jesus' declaration, "I am the bread of life" (John 6:35).

A common family dish consisted of a kind of meat and vegetable stew. Each one helped himself from the common dish by a spoon or scoop formed by a piece of bread freshly torn from the loaf. It was an act of courtesy and a means of reassurance of friendship to prepare such a "sop" and hand it to the next at the table (John 13:26).

The chief meal time came just after sunset with the day's work done. The toilers from the field had trudged home. It was a time of family reunion. Cushions were placed on the floor around a low table. Amid the joys of family the one hot-cooked meal of the day was consumed. Following supper, hands were washed by pouring water over them from a brass container.

Children were a delight to the Palestinian home. Homelife was happy, and family ties were strong. All understood the significance of Jesus' words when He spoke of "a house divided against itself, that house cannot stand" (Mark 3:23–25). Few toys were provided, although archaeologists have uncovered such items as a child's doll, ball, and tools. They amused themselves during occasions when the adults were otherwise occupied, such as at funerals and weddings (Matthew 11:16, 17). Children were taught to honor their parents, part of which duty was the care of the aged. Jesus roundly rebuked the casuistry of the Pharisees in permitting the money that should have gone for the care of parents to be "dedicated" to the Temple. This practice of "corban" Jesus attacked as a means of sidestepping normal family responsibility (Mark 7:11–13).

An important part of the child's education took place in the home. From the time of Moses, moral and religious instruction was an important feature of family life (Deuteronomy 6:1–9). The advent of the synagogue as a formal training institution outside the home still did not displace the role of the parents in the discipline and training of the young. Jesus was reared in a home where important values were communicated (Luke 2:51). In addition to the moral training which the Law demanded for parents, each father was required to see that his son learned a trade. Without doubt Jesus learned carpentry from Joseph (Matthew 13:55).

Social Life

Although Palestine was largely an agricultural economy, the people lived in towns and villages. Farmers and shepherds had homes in the community, in spite of the fact that daily they had to journey, often great distances, to their outlying fields. The houses of the village were often so close together that robbers could run from rooftop to rooftop. And the people were just as close as their houses. Consider the sense of neighborliness in the story of the lost coin—the neighbors and friends made the episode a cause for a neighborhood party (Luke 15:8–10). The same common joy was experienced when the shepherd found the one stray sheep (Luke 15:3–7).

Not everything was pleasant in the Palestinian villages and towns. Sanitary conditions were primitive. The citizens of the first century carried canes through the narrow streets as an indispensable protection against the ever-present lean and hungry dogs. In our society, we think of dogs as family pets. In the ancient Near East, however, dogs were the scavengers who lived off the refuse that was thrown into the streets. Jesus said in Matthew 7:6, "Give not that which is holy unto the dogs," probably referring to the meat used in the Temple sacrifices. In Mark 7:28, Jesus alludes to the dogs eating crumbs from the table in his conversation with the Syrophoenician woman. The story of Lazarus in Luke 16 indicates that the beggar ate with the dogs the crumbs from the rich man's table. Evidently napkins as we know them were not used, but in that day people ate with their hands and cleaned them by wiping them on pieces of bread which were then discarded. This discarded bread is probably what Lazarus lived on.

Jesus commanded great fame, first in Galilee, then later in Judea, as the word spread about His power to deliver people from disease. The Near East has from time immemorial been ridden with disease. Mark 5:26 records the sad tale of the woman "who had suffered many things of many physicians, and had spent all that she had . . . " The "physicians" were self-appointed experts who dabbled in sorcery, such as Simon of Acts 8:9. The rabbis occasionally served as "physicians." Bleeding of the ill was a common prescribed remedy, a service rendered by the local barber. Little was known of medicine as we think of it, and many people lived in great suffering. Little wonder it was that when the Great Physician drew near, the crowds thrilled at the news, for He had genuine power to heal people afflicted with demons and disease. Today the Great Physician is still healing the sick. And, even more wonderful, He is healing broken souls and lives.

The people of the Near East have always placed great importance on hospitality, The Bedouin of the desert who took a wayfaring stranger into his tent was honor-bound to protect that person from injury for as long as he was his guest. David's words, "Thou preparest a table for me in the presence of mine enemies" (Psalm 23:5) seem to allude to this deep tradition of Eastern hospitality. On the other hand, for a stranger to decline an invitation to partake of hospitality was considered quite rude. Because the exchange of acts of hospitality could be very time-consuming, the admonition of the Lord to the disciples being sent on their first mission, "Salute no man on his way" (Luke 10:4), makes considerable sense. This was not just a mere "How do you do" that those on God's business had to avoid.

Jesus considered the care of strangers and the needy to be an important mark of the genuine disciple. "For I was an hungered, and ye gave me meat: I was thirsty, and ye gave me drink: I was a stranger, and ye took me in" (Matthew 25:35). The act of giving a cup of cold water was recognition by the host that the stranger was considered a worthy person (Matthew 10:42). For a stranger to ask for a cup of cold water was an invitation to friendship. This would account for the shock of the woman to whom Jesus ministered at the well, for the Jews were alienated from the Samaritans (John 4:7–9). The episode recounted by Jesus in Luke 11:5–8 takes on considerable significance when one realizes that the Palestinian disliked very much to be disturbed after having retired, and hospitality was not normally extended after the evening meal. For the friend to get up and give the latecomer the loaves at such a late hour was a most unusual breach of local custom. The point Jesus sought to make, of course, is that if an earthly friend would break tradition for an importunate supplicator, how much more is our heavenly Father disposed to respond to our cries.

Funerals were important social occasions for the Jews. Friends and neighbors were expected to participate in honoring the deceased by public mournings. Usually it was on the same day as the death occurred that the body was prepared for burying and carried on an open bier to the place of interment. As the sorrowing company made its way to the final resting place, all who met the procession were expected to join it, adding their wails to the doleful group. It was customary to display grief by tearing the hair and clothing and to beat the breast with loud cries of anguish (Mark 5:38). Jesus encountered such a procession emerging from the gate of the city of Nain, but when the dead youth was raised through the mighty power of God their sorrow was turned to a tumult of rejoicing and worship (Luke 7:11–17). In Galilee, the incident in which the daughter of Jairus was healed discloses a strange occurrence. To our thinking, it would be somewhat disconcerting to discover the wailing of the mourners so suddenly converted into laughter (Luke 8:53). However, in the ancient Near East it was quite common to employ professional mourners to swell the sound of sorrow, as a tribute to the departed. These were usually aged women, often widows. It was not uncommon for the tears of the mourners to be preserved and kept in bottles as a kind of memorial (Psalm 56:8).

Without question the most important social event in the life of the Palestinian Jews was the marriage ceremony. Marriage was really considered to have three phases. First, it was common for parents to arrange the marriage of daughters extremely early, even in infancy. However upon arrival at marriageable age, the wishes of the children were usually respected. Hence, such early parental arrangements were quite tentative and were easily broken. It really betokened the feeling of responsibility on the part of the parents that they find suitable partners for their children. Much more important was the second phase, the betrothal, or engagement. This was considered as sacred as the marriage itself, and could be broken only by securing a written divorce document. Such an engagement normally lasted a year, and then was followed by the festive marriage ceremony itself. In the impending birth of Jesus, Joseph was faced with a serious dilemma. Mary, to whom he was betrothed but not married, was with child. He, being an upright and honorable Jew, was expected to "put her away," or obtain a divorce, thus preserving his own honor and maintaining a high standard of morality for the community. He loved Mary, and wished if he had to do this to do it as quietly as possible, so as to spare her all the embarrassment he could. It was at this critical moment in Joseph's soul-searching that the angel of the Lord came with the breathtaking news that Mary was miraculously with child. She, a virgin of Israel, was to bear the Son of God (Matthew 1:18–21).

The wedding ceremony itself was usually conducted in the home of the bridegroom. During the day the bride was taken to the home of the groom, where assisted by her attendants the time was spent in arranging her garments. As the evening wore on, the invited women guests fussed about the bride, and spent their time in appropriate light conversation, and partaking of refreshments. It was not uncommon for the women to become weary during the long hours of waiting and for some to fall asleep. Meanwhile, the groom had been spending the day at the home of a relative. About sunset his male friends began to gather, following the day's work. They had already had a quick supper, and came to spend the evening in a kind of "bachelor's party," before escorting the groom to his home where the wedding was to take place. About an hour before midnight the men left with the groom. Torches would light the procession, and each man carried his own candle. The brilliant spectacle attracted the villagers along the way, and one can imagine the excited people crowding balconies and rooftops along the streets to catch a glimpse of the procession. Further down the street, the cry would rise, "He is coming! He is coming!" for all eyes are focused on the bridegroom. At the home where the bride and her friends had been waiting, as the hour approached, the lamps were lit. Out into the street a short way the maidens went with joy to welcome the groom. The invited guests thereupon went into the marriage feast and the door was shut, the rest of the throng dispersing to their homes. How significant to the people of that day was the tale of the wise and the foolish virgins (Matthew 25:1–13). With the coming of the Bridegroom so very near, how we need to be careful that we have oil in our lamps! He is coming!

Again, one can appreciate Jesus' comments regarding "the children of the bridechamber" as being the invited wedding guests (Matthew 9:15). Also, it was on the wedding feast, and only on that occasion, that the bride appeared with her hair let down. For women to appear publicly in this fashion on any other occasion was considered immoral. Observe then how the Pharisee despised the woman who used her hair to dry the feet of Jesus (Luke 7:36–50). Jesus did not cast her out, as Simon thought He should, but He forgave her sins that day, and taught a lesson in compassion to His disciples.

The World of Work

Much of the imagery that Jesus employed in His language

came directly from the daily tasks in which the people of the land engaged. Theirs was a life of toil, chiefly centered in the rural occupations of primitive farming and shepherding. Day was reckoned from sunup to sundown, the first hour beginning with dawn, the twelfth hour reckoned at sunset. In that latitude the variation from season to season is quite limited, so there is a relatively constant amount of daylight. Matthew 20:1–16 recounts the story of the vineyard laborers, some of whom were hired shortly before sunset, about the eleventh hour, and yet who received the same wage as those who had toiled through the heat of the midday. Normally the workday consisted of twelve hours of hard toil. The same passage begins with the account of the householder who went out to hire laborers for his vineyard early in the morning. Each day at dawn the local villagers who depended on hiring out as laborers for a livelihood gathered at the recognized village centers with their tools, waiting for a wealthy landowner to hire them for that day.

In that climate there was sowing or harvesting, pruning, or plowing to do throughout much of the year. Early wheat and barley were sown in the fall, and the plowing was done then, too. During the winter months of December and January the citrus fruits ripened and the vineyards demanded pruning. Rainfall was more plentiful then, and the weather cooled, with snow falling on the highest elevations. The showers that came in the spring, about April, were called "the latter rain," and this moisture was urgently needed for the maturing of the wheat and barley crops. Without the "latter rain" the harvest would be meager or nil. For God to have His desired harvest in our lives, we too need the latter rain of His Holy Spirit to nourish our lives!

With May comes the long dry season and the early harvest-time. Almonds, apricots, and plums ripen, too. By August the threshing is about finished, and the grape season arrives. Figs and other fruit mature at this time, as well. October is the time for the completion of the grape and fig harvest and for the gathering of olives. This is the time of the "early rain" (also called the "former rain"), softening the sun-baked soil for the fall plowing.

A common sight was the sower (Matthew 13:3). One can easily imagine the various types of soil depicted in the passage, all in one location—some rich, some thinly covering a shelf of limestone, and between the various patches of field, the pathway that served as a divider in lieu of fences. The grain as it ripened might grow out over the pathways. Jewish law (Deuteronomy 23:25) permitted passersby to help themselves to the grain that could easily be reached from the pathway, without fear of being considered thieves—it was a common courtesy. It was not this that the disciples were criticized for, but because they did it on the Sabbath (Matthew 12:1, 2).

The vineyards produced poor crops about every third or fourth year. Wise farmers spaced fig and olive trees throughout the vineyard so that in the event of a poor grape yield they would still have something to harvest. Such plots were called "gardens." These could be found outside village and town. The Garden of Gethsemane that Jesus enjoyed as He journeyed between Bethany and Jerusalem was just such an agricultural arrangement.

Who can picture ancient Palestine without considering the shepherd? Few illustrations of the loving care of our heavenly Father are more appropriate than that of the tenderness with which the shepherd cared for his sheep. A common size flock for the shepherd was about one hundred sheep, which accords well with the story of the good shepherd who had ninety-nine, and went to look for the lost one (Luke 15:3–7). While he searched the highland meadows for the stray, the rest of the sheep were probably being cared for by another guardian, for it was not uncommon for more than one shepherd to watch a single flock. Quite possibly the sheep were in the "sheepfold" (John 10:1), a cave, or a stone-walled enclosure with a single entrance. In a given village, all the flocks might be given shelter during the night in such a sheepfold. In the morning each shepherd would call out his own sheep, for they learned to know the voice of their particular shepherd (John 10:3). Each morning they eagerly followed him, for they knew he had come to lead them out into pasture for the day. Can one imagine a more impressive picture of the love of God to us than that of the Good Shepherd who laid down His life for His sheep?

Palestine in Jesus' day was not only a rural countryside preoccupied with agricultural pursuits. Villages and cities were crowded with open-air stalls of every description, where farmers sold their produce, or money changers did a banking business. Peddlers, merchants, small-craft shops, all vied with one another for the attention of the crowds that flowed through the narrow, congested streets. One can imagine the confusion of sounds and smells that must have filled the air.

Rabbinical tradition required each young man to learn a trade. Such crafts were usually carried on at home, although because of the heat such work was actually performed outdoors in the courtyard. One such craft common in that day was the weaving and dyeing of cloth. Some men were skilled masons, and were called upon as the local experts when building projects in the village were undertaken. That climate demanded a solid foundation so that the alternating dry and wet seasons would not crack the walls. Hence great care was expended in getting down to the bedrock, often at considerable expense. Jesus mentions the wise mason who built his house on a rock (Matthew 7:24). Other craftsmen common in that day were the potters, the carpenters, and the metalworkers. Jesus called a variety of men to be His disciples, one of whom worked as a tax collector, or "publican" (Matthew 10:3). It is possible that Matthew was a toll-collector on one of the great commercial routes, collecting revenue for the despised Romans. How wonderful that Jesus could use even a social outcast.

One occupation that commands considerable attention in the Gospel narratives is fishing. The disciples worked more as commercial fishermen than in any other line of activity. Thus we hear the call of the Master ringing, "I will make you fishers of men!"

The Sea of Galilee abounded in fish, and furnished one of the chief industries for that province. The towns that dotted the

Galilean shore were fishing centers. Bethsaida, the town in which Peter, Andrew, and Philip lived, meant "House of Fishes." The commercial fisheries transported their products to Jerusalem and other metropolitan centers. Some scholars are inclined to feel that the familiarity of John with the city of Jerusalem, which his Gospel discloses, suggests that he handled the Jerusalem retail outlet of the Galilean fishing company, while his brother James, and possibly Peter and Andrew, operated the Galilean end.

Summary

In clear and simple language Jesus spoke wonderful truths of eternal value to the people of Palestine. He spoke about domestic matters familiar to them all. He spoke about social customs with which they were entirely familiar. The soil and the marketplace furnished illustrations and figures to punctuate His message.

Jesus lived with those He loved. He took great pains to choose just the right words to emphasize the eternal truths. His intense desire was to see lives changed. One must wonder whether we have really discharged our responsibility to our neighbor until we, too, have sought to find the key that will unlock his heart.

---

[1]Joseph L. Gift, *Life and Customs in Jesus' Time* (Cincinnati: The Standard Publishing Foundation, 1957).

[2]G. M. Mackie, *Bible Manners and Customs* (New York: Fleming H. Revell Company, n.d.).

7

A Nation Scattered and Mixed

Of the four to five million Jews living during the earthly life of Jesus by far the greater number lived outside Palestine. These were the Jews of the Dispersion, or as it is sometimes called, the Diaspora. Within Palestine there was an additional complication. Not all who lived there were Jews. Notable groups who had their own separate communities within Palestine were the Greeks and the Samaritans. Although the principal ministry of Jesus was to the Palestinian Jews, there are important implications for our understanding of the New Testament in these other groups.

The Dispersion

During the ninth century B.C. there is a faint allusion to a Jewish colony having been established at Damascus in Syria (1 Kings 20:34). This seems to be the earliest evidence of Jewish transplantation. However, such voluntary emigration was succeeded in the next centuries by enforced mass deportations of inhabitants from both the Northern Kingdom and from Judah as the hand of judgment fell on the idolatrous people of God. The Assyrians and the Babylonians made a practice of stripping subjugated territories of the local leadership and skilled craftsmen, in one stroke rendering the conquered nation helpless to organize a successful revolution and also pumping fresh blood into their own homeland. Apparently many of those who had been so uprooted when the Northern Kingdom of Israel fell in 721 B.C. lost their national and spiritual identity. They just melted into the vastness of Assyria. Many of the rest who remained in the land intermarried with the local people.

The same was not true, however, of the Southern Kingdom. Several important factors contributed to the retention of their integrity during the Babylonian Captivity. One was the powerful preaching of God's great spokesmen, notably the prophets Ezekiel and Daniel. Another factor was the rise of the synagogue as a means for keeping the worship of God fresh among the people week by week, in spite of the cessation of Temple sacrifice.

The result of this was that when Cyrus the Mede granted permission for the exiles to return to their Palestinian homeland, a sizable group responded to Zerubbabel's challenge, but an even larger number decided to stay on in Babylon. These Jews in Babylon had found that they could maintain their distinctive religious tradition and had found a measure of acceptance in an alien land. It was easier for them to stay on there than to pull up roots to return to their devastated homeland. The Babylonian Jews maintained their identity for more than a thousand years. After the destruction of the Jerusalem Temple in A.D. 70, the rabbinical tradition was kept alive in the East, an impressive "Babylonian Talmud" testifying to the continuing vigor of Judaism far from home.

Another aspect of the Dispersion enters the picture with the advent of Greek dominion in the Near East in the fourth century B.C. Quite possibly the unification of the Mediterranean world, making commerce and trade between scattered areas more convenient, was the important inducement to attract commercially minded Jews to make new homes for themselves along the trade routes of the empire. The Jews developed a reputation as excellent colonists. Both Seleucid and Ptolemaic monarchs offered special advantages to Jews who would leave Palestine for areas that needed colonizing.

The city of Alexandria in Egypt soon boasted a Jewish population estimated to exceed one million. Far up the Nile, near the present location of the great Aswan Dam, there existed an island colony of Jews who left behind a body of literature that has been discovered only in the last several decades. These "Elephantine papyri," named after the island in the Nile, have shed considerable light on the life and outlook of the Egyptian contingent of the Jews of the Dispersion, dating back as far as the fifth century B.C. The Jews there evidently were not so definite in their maintenance of the Mosaic law. Egyptian Jews had their own temples, in sharp contradiction to the severe denunciation of such practices in the Book of Deuteronomy. Some pagan elements unfortunately got mixed into the pure worship of the Israelites in Egypt.

During the time of the ascendancy of the Roman Empire, beginning with the century before Jesus, the Jews spread rapidly through the Mediterranean world. Syria had numerous cities with large Jewish sections in them. Asia Minor (modern Turkey) had more than seventy cities boasting a Jewish colony. It was to Jewish Christians there that Peter addressed his first epistle. Even the capital of the empire, Rome itself, quite early had a Jewish population. The expulsion of Jews from Rome that affected Aquila and Priscilla, mentioned in Acts 18:2, was preceded by earlier expulsions dating as far back as 139 B.C. However, the Jews, unpopular as they were for their unusual religious practices, considered barbaric by the pagans, managed to return again and again to Rome.

The Jews had a reputation for exclusiveness—they neither participated in the vile amusements of the day nor engaged in the common public pagan worship ceremonies. The Jews in their unwillingness to compromise created an air of tension with their pagan neighbors. It was this smoldering hostility that erupted periodically in the expulsions from the capital. However, the Romans recognized great moral quality in the Jews, nonetheless, and were willing to make special concessions to them. They alone of all the peoples of the Roman Empire enjoyed the status of exemption from state-worship, an evil practice of which we shall speak later. Because the Jewish law forbade extensive traveling on the Sabbath, they were exempt from military service. Some Jews did join the army, and in this fashion earned the coveted Roman citizenship. It is considered possible by scholars that it was through this means that Paul's father became a citizen of the empire.

It is quite likely that many Jews living in a world dominated by pagan culture far from the shadow of their Jerusalem Temple, compromised and thus lost their traditional Mosaic faith. Most of them, however, did adhere with rigid and vigorous discipline to Judaism. As many as could traveled periodically back to Jerusalem for the annual feasts. The Temple tax of half a shekel a year was faithfully paid by rigorous worshipers across the expanse of the empire. Utterly strategic in their ability to maintain their heritage generation after generation was the ever-present synagogue. In every city throughout the Mediterranean world where there were at least ten adult male Jews, a synagogue was established. It was the faithful reading of the Law and the maintenance of prayer in the synagogue that kept their religious life aflame. In the plan of God these synagogues became the steppingstones for evangelizing the first century world in the day of the apostles. How often Paul opened his citywide evangelistic crusade in the local synagogue, occasioning either a revival or a riot—and frequently both!

Although Jesus never traveled beyond the borders of Palestine, He undoubtedly ministered to many Jews of the Dispersion who made the pilgrimage to Jerusalem. They constituted such a sizable portion of the "lost sheep of the house of Israel" that one can be sure that the Great Shepherd bore a great burden for them to share the light of the gospel. In the providence of God, the Early Church found the scattered synagogues flung across the world of that day to be the means of fulfilling the commission of our Lord, "to the Jew first, and also to the Greek." The apostles had no difficulty in preaching Jesus as the promised Messiah, using the Old Testament as their sermon material.

The Samaritans

In central Palestine, about thirty miles north of the city of Jerusalem, there still survive about 300 Samaritans, the last of a once thriving society. They reside in the shadow of their sacred shrine, Mount Gerizim, in Nablus, the site of the ancient city of Shechem. In the days of Jesus the Samaritans controlled the area surrounding the city of Samaria, an area that lay directly between the Jewish provinces of Galilee to the north and Judea to the south. Although the Galileans usually took the direct route through Samaria on their journeys to the capital in Judea, there was such deep hostility between Jews and Samaritans that Judeans frequently took the far more circuitous route to Galilee by way of Perea, far to the east across the Jordan valley.

John 4:4 contains the expression, "And he must needs go through Samaria." Jesus had been ministering in Judea, but now wished to return to Galilee. Possibly He wished to avoid the region of Perea, governed by Herod Antipas, or it may be that the Master was willing to risk the displeasure of the Samaritans to seek out a hungering soul of whom He had supernatural foreknowledge. In any event, Jesus encountered the woman at the well not far from Shechem. She was apparently alone, drawing water at noon, shunned by the other village women who wanted nothing to do with her, for undoubtedly her sordid moral reputation had made her an outcast fit only to draw water in the heat of the day when the others were not at the well. Hers is a picture of desolation and misery. No wonder that she was astonished that Jesus, a Jew, would bother to talk with her, a Samaritan, and a woman of the streets. What compassion this episode displays! Tenderly Jesus spoke to her of "worship in spirit and in truth," avoiding the harsh argumentation of centuries between the Jews and the Samaritans that centered on which mountain was the sacred templesite ordained of God—Mount Zion in Jerusalem or Mount Gerizim. He spoke to her of "living water" that would quench the soulthirst that parched her so. The result of that remarkable encounter was a two-day revival meeting. Although Jesus concentrated on reaching the Jews first, He challenged His apostles, following the Resurrection, to preach to the Samaritans, but first they were to wait in Jerusalem for the enduement of

Pentecostal power as the necessary spiritual equipment for this important assignment (Acts 1:8).

From whence were these Samaritans? It seems most likely that their origin is related to the destruction of the Northern Kingdom and the fall of its capital, Samaria, in 721 B.C. The Assyrians had denuded the land of its best citizens, leaving, however, a sizable remnant to care for the land. This remnant evidently intermarried with local pagan people, and possibly with some foreigners who drifted into the land in the years that followed. By the time of the return from Babylonian exile in the time of Zerubbabel two hundred years later, they had a reputation of being a mixed race and worse, having a corrupted form of religion. The opposition to rebuilding the Temple which so discouraged the people seems to have stemmed from Samaria, in part at least. A few years later, in the time of Ezra and Nehemiah, the enmity that the returning exiles had incurred from the Samaritans seems to have deepened. Nehemiah deported the grandson of the high priest for marrying Sanballat's daughter.

It was probably about this time that the Samaritans built a rival temple of their own on Mount Gerizim. Through the years they developed their own "doctored" version of the Pentateuch, which gave apparent Mosaic sanction to their Gerizim site. The rest of the Old Testament they rejected. During the time of the Maccabean revolt, John Hyrcanus forced them to give up idolatry and destroyed their temple, which was never rebuilt. Their center of worship was maintained in Shechem.

By the time of Jesus, a profound hatred had grown up between Jew and Samaritan. The Samaritans on occasion sneaked into Jerusalem to desecrate the Temple area. They sometimes were hostile to Jews traveling through their own countryside. On the other hand, the Jews despised the Samaritans, considering them to be almost as bad as Gentiles, or pagans. John 8:48 discloses this foul feeling that existed, for the Jews acidly abused Jesus, "Say we not well that thou art a Samaritan, and hast a devil?" Imagine what a shattering experience it was for the Jews to hear the story of the Good Samaritan, recounted by Jesus in Luke 10! The Pharisees would not even use the name Samaritan, preferring to use the derogatory title "Cuthim," which emphasized the foreign character of the people. The love of Jesus for the despised, the downtrodden, the rejected of His day was like a breath of pure air in that hate-filled land.

The Palestinian Greeks

Within Palestine there was not only the problem of the Samaritans for the Jews, but there were in addition a number of Greek cities, populated in part by Gentiles whom the Jews abhorred. About the year 200 B.C., during the time of Greek power, several cities south and east of the Sea of Galilee were built and populated by Greeks. Shortly after the birth of Christ these cities formed a league, primarily for trade, but also for defense since they were like a cluster of islands in a Semitic sea. Originally there were ten cities in the league, hence the name "Decapolis," meaning "ten cities." The Romans permitted them almost complete independence during the time of Christ, each city having its own separate senate to govern it, quite unlike the Jewish state that looked to Jerusalem as its central capital.

In addition to these early Greek cities, during the time of the Herods several cities were either built or rebuilt as Greek cities. Among many others, these included Caesarea on the Mediterranean coast, Samaria which was renamed Sebaste in honor of the Emperor Augustus, and Tiberias, the town situated on the Sea of Galilee. The Herods engaged in this building enterprise with the blessing of the Romans, for they wished to stimulate Greco-Roman culture in the heartland of the Jews hoping thereby to break down their exclusivism. The Jews who had resisted Hellenization since the time of the Greek supremacy had developed an extremely hostile feeling toward this encroachment into their land. The rabbis arranged elaborate means for maintaining complete separation between Jew and Gentile. Jewish horror of the Gentile had as its foundation the fear of contamination by idolators. The mere touch of a pagan on a cask of wine polluted it. There were none but the most necessary dealings with the despised Gentiles. Yet, Jesus challenged the disciples, who were of course Jews, to proclaim the Good News to all the world (Matthew 28:19).

During the early Galilean ministry of Jesus, inhabitants of the Decapolis area joined the throngs to hear His wonderful word (Matthew 4:25). On another occasion Jesus crossed the Sea of Galilee to the southeast shore, stopping in the region near Gadara, where He wonderfully delivered the demoniac (Mark 5:1–20). The reference to many swine there further emphasizes the non-Jewish character of the area. Later in His ministry Jesus made at least one tour through the Decapolis area. The one instance recorded in which Jesus apparently actually visited the cities of that region is found in Mark 7:31.

In that day, the high ethical standards of the Jew so far outshone the corrupt and vile pagan world that some pagans became proselytes to Judaism. Evidently the Greeks mentioned by John (John 12:20) were just such converts to Judaism who had undergone instruction, been circumcised, received the baptism ceremony reserved for proselytes, and offered sacrifices in the Temple. Others were "half-proselytes," Greeks who went to the synagogue, honored the Law, but did not submit to circumcision. Some think these were titled "God-fearers." Quite possibly Cornelius (Acts 10:2) was a half-proselyte from the pagan world. Surely God is no respecter of persons, for a mighty Pentecostal revival came to the home of Cornelius, who to the Jews was a mere second-class citizen.

Summary

In God's providence the Jews were scattered widely through the whole of the Roman Empire by the time of Christ and the apostles. The ability of the Jews to maintain their study of the Old Testament Scriptures in the synagogues they erected wherever they dwelt became the primary means by which the gospel was to spill over into the entire Mediterranean world during the first century. "To the Jew first" was the mandate of Christ, and proved to be an effective means for dispersing the message of salvation, even though few Jews themselves responded.

In Palestine the sharp and bitter hatred of the Jews for their near neighbors, the Samaritans and the Greeks, was put to shame by the compassion of Jesus, for Jesus demonstrated His love even for the despised of Palestinian society.

8

The Pagan World

As Jesus journeyed through Palestine, He must have seen numerous temples and shrines dedicated to the worship of pagan deities in the Greco-Roman cities. Only Judea itself was exempt from this defilement. Jesus' first followers were almost exclusively Jews, but after Pentecost, the Spirit-baptized Church would clash head on with the pagan world in fulfillment of Jesus' challenge to disciple "all nations" (Matthew 28:19). Paul confronted Greek philosophers at Athens (Acts 17:18). At Ephesus he bore the wrath of devotees of the local mystery cult dedicated to Artemis (Acts 19:23–41). The world of Jesus' day was a very religious world, but its inhabitants had a heart-hunger that ritual and pageantry could not satisfy. In truth Jesus came at the fullness of time (Galatians 4:4), for the gospel preached by the apostles of the first century gathered a rich harvest throughout the Empire among the Gentiles whose religious world was so very empty.

The Greek Mind

About the time that Ezra was recalling the Jews to a spiritual renewal in Judea following the return of the Babylonian exiles, there began to flourish in the city of Athens a "golden age" of great thinkers. The philosophers Socrates, Plato, and Aristotle, with several lesser lights, constituted the most noble attempt of the human mind to discover meaning and purpose in this world and how to live properly. But this was precisely the problem. Man in his disordered state since the fall of Adam has been so diseased by the effects of sin (Romans 1–3) that he cannot find the truth without outside assistance. God sent just such a shaft of light to the world through His prophets, and finally, the brightness of Light itself in Jesus of Nazareth, the full and final Revelation of a concerned and compassionate God (Hebrews 1:1,2). As noble as have been the best attempts of man to arrange his own systems of ideas of morality and religion, the attempt has proved to be a tragic failure. One cannot climb to God by unaided human efforts; he must first admit his own darkness and need. Religion is the attempt of man to search for God; Christianity is the disclosure that God has been looking for man. It is interesting to observe that many of the so-called modern philosophies that crop up in our own society seem to bear a startling resemblance to the ideas advanced by the ancient Greeks. There really is not too much that is so new under the sun, after all.

Platonism. The most famous of the ancient philosophers was Plato of Athens, who founded a famous school known as the Academy, about 400 B.C. The closing of the Academy in A.D. 529 by the Christian Emperor Justinian is used by many scholars as a symbolic dividing line between the periods of ancient and medieval history, symbolizing also the triumph of Christianity over ancient paganism. For Plato, the real world was a world of ideas, or concepts, the highest of which is the idea of the Good, the True, and the Beautiful. The world in which we dwell was but a shadow of the idea which lies behind it. In effect, then, material things, including the human body, were a kind of prison for man. His hope for release from the unreal world of material things lay in contemplation and meditation. For Plato, God was an impersonal "idea," salvation lay in correct thinking. Plato had no solution for the problem of sin; he made the fatal mistake of assuming that if people only knew to do right they would have sense enough to do right.

There have been twentieth-century people with the same naive view regarding sin—those who have assumed that telling people how they ought to behave will automatically produce the desired effects. The "social gospel" of the early years of the century was deeply imbued with such an unrealistic and na-ively optimistic view of unregenerate human nature. We know, of course, that without Christ's deliverance from the power of sin man will not do right even when he knows to do right.

Gnosticism. A whole series of systems and diverse move-ments that spanned the time of Jesus was Gnosticism, usually a blending of Greek and Oriental ideas, sometimes mixed with Judaism and later with Christianity. There was no single founder nor was there a precise form to this strange and pow-erful influence in the ancient world. No other force was a greater threat to the Early Church. Paul seems to have Gnosticism in mind as he writes Colossians. John's Gospel and First Epistle reflect the battle that was raging toward the end of the first century.

Gnosticism derives its name from *gnosis,* the Greek word for "knowledge." The Gnostics claimed "special knowledge" which those who desired salvation must attain from them. They alone were "in the know." Like the Platonists, they conceived of mat-ter as being of less value than things immaterial. In fact, they held the God of the creation to be a lesser deity than the Su-preme God, for they could not believe that a good God could be involved in making material things, such as bodies, which they regarded as evil. Again, like the Platonists, they held contem-plation to be important for releasing the soul from the prison of the body, and thus to be united with the host of other released spirits.

The Gnostic spirit that troubled the people of the ancient world appears in our day from time to time. Those who attach non-Biblical conditions to salvation, who say that one cannot understand the Bible without their particular interpretation, are really very much like the Gnostics of old.

Epicureanism. Unlike Plato, whose abstract reasoning was beyond the reach of the common people, Epicurus was a "com-mon sense" philosopher. He too founded a school in Athens, about a hundred years after Plato. For him, Truth was not some absolute, abstract idea "out there," but was to be defined in terms of one's own senses and perceptions. Wisdom lies in the pursuit of pleasure, which Epicurus defined as the absence of pain. Contrary to common belief Epicurus was a man of noble concern. He did not advocate sensual lust and gluttonous behavior at all. However, his ideas led to unbridled selfishness. His system had the fatal flaw of placing man and his pleasures in the center of the picture. There was no room in such a scene for God. Every man did that which was pleasurable in his own eyes. Physical death is the end of the road for them. In today's world, those whose real god is the pursuit of pleasure expose themselves as children of Epicurus of old.

Stoicism. About the same time as Epicurus, a thinker named Zeno attracted a following in Athens, lecturing to his disciples under a covered porch, or *stoa,* hence the name "Stoic." Zeno was in sharp disagreement with the Epicureans, who were practical atheists and who leaned toward self-indulgence. For the Stoics, there was an ultimate beyond this world, a divine reason, which was an impersonal force much like Plato's concept of the Absolute Idea. Man's duty was to live in harmony with this Reason, or Natural Law. Duty and will are superior to emotion, so that man even in the face of stress could rise above his circumstances in which he is a prisoner. This he does by resoluteness and fortitude. The self-controlled man was the free man. In spite of the nobility of this ideal Stoicism was a barren philosophy, for life was a grim round of duty impossible of attainment for all but a few. It represented the religion of the self-righteous who feel that they are able to live by their own code of morality without divine assistance. There are a host in today's world who are quite proud of their morality. Theirs is a religion without Christ, cold, frequently selfish, and all but impervious to an awareness of sin.

Cynicism and Skepticism. These two movements typify the despair to which unaided human reason must eventually lead. The movement of Cynicism is best known through Diogenes, a fourth century B.C. eccentric who lived in a large tub. His despair at the impossibility of finding true values and genuine objectives in life led him to the conclusion that real peace could come only through eliminating all desires. His modern counterpart is found in the hippie who spurns what he considers to be the hollowness of values in his society. But with nothing more constructive to offer, he simply reverts to a virtual animal-level of existence. His is a kind of protest against the darkness without and the despair within his soul.

The Skeptics share in common with the Cynics the rejection of the possibility of man's finding absolute values. They were perceptive enough to discern that knowledge depends on human opinions, there can never be assurance of having arrived at ultimate truth, for the opinions of men are so varied. Pyrrho of Elis, who lived about three hundred years before Christ, was the founder of this movement. He was suspicious of anyone who claimed to have the key to Truth. His watchword was "suspended judgment." In today's world, it is the essence of academic fashion to be suspicious of all that purports to be fact. The Christian at the university of today must bear the scorn and the ridicule of his associates who cannot understand the joy he experiences when he sings with conviction, "I *know* Whom I have believed." Jesus is still speaking with authority today, and not as the scribes of this world!

The Mystery Religions

By the time of Christ the failure of the greatest minds, the ancient Greek philosophers, to resolve the deep yearning in the human heart, had led to general agnosticism. The pagan world had become a virtual religious vacuum. Into this vacuum there swept a number of weird cults, mostly of Middle Eastern origin, whose vows of secrecy seemed to heighten popular fascination for them. These "mystery religions" were flourishing at the time of Christ and represented a genuine rivalry in the Gentile world to the message of His apostles. Sometimes these cults were limited in influence to a local community, where a shrine was erected, although some had a much wider influence. These cults were an attempt to offer the people a kind of personal religion which they craved and which the bankrupt Greek philosophies denied to them.

Eleusis. The oldest mystery cult of all was centered at Eleusis, a small town near Athens. Here was reenacted each year a series of sacred rites based on an ancient Greek myth that was really an attempt to explain the yearly cycle of changing seasons. Following an elaborate preparation of candidates, a series of initiation rites, processions, and sacrifices was conducted by the priesthood. The culmination each year of the "mysteries" was a sacred drama reenacting the story of the myth on which the cult was based. This occurred in a great hall at Eleusis each September. As the priests performed this "sacred drama" the faithful observers were expected to experience a kind of vicarious involvement in the drama, an experience that was to fill an emotional need not met by the philosophies. There is a striking resemblance between such a "mystery religion" and many of the lodges of our day which are really a pseudoreligion, complete with secret rites of initiation.

Mithra. If the Eleusinian mysteries were the oldest of the cults, Mithraism was the most widespread. Its membership was limited to men. It was widespread in the Roman army. It had no priestly caste, as did most of the mystery cults, its rites being performed by those who had achieved the seventh, the highest degree of status within the ranks. The worship ceremonies occurred in underground caves, each of which contained a statue of Mithra, the sun-god, pictured as slaying a bull. Evidently this was to symbolize his mastery over evil and darkness. Although details of their practices are not clear, the rite of initiation appears to have involved the slaying of a bull over the naked body of the candidate in such a way that the blood poured over him. In the course of this gruesome ceremony the initiate was to drink some of the blood, thereby gaining the courage and strength of the bull.

Isis and Osiris. This cult originated in Egypt. Like the Eleusinian mysteries it was centered on the reenactment of an ancient myth which promised immortality to the participants. In the myth, Osiris is murdered, but through the magical rites performed by his consort, Isis, he is restored to life. Chapels dedicated to this cult sprang up throughout the Mediterranean world, particularly appealing to women. During the period of Greek influence in Egypt the cult was modified considerably, with Osiris being retitled Serapis. During the time of Jesus the worship of Isis and Serapis was widespread.

Cybele. A particularly distasteful cult was that dedicated to the worship of Cybele. This cult originated in the Middle East, and by the time of Christ was well-established throughout the Roman Empire. It centered on the reenactment of a restoration myth. A shepherd boy named Attis died, but his goddess consort, Cybele, or "the Great Mother," restored him to life again. The annual ritual, conducted each spring by the followers of this cult, was characterized by wild frenzy in which the participants cut themselves with knives, sprinkling their own blood on the altars. As with many of the mystery cults, gross immorality was involved.

Emperor Worship

For many years the Greeks had ascribed supernatural powers to their leaders, calling them "Lord" or Savior. In various ways, in spite of the fact that the Romans had conquered the Greek world, Greek ideas successfully infiltrated the Roman Empire. The worship of the emperor was one such cultural intrusion. It was in the reign of Augustus, the emperor during the time when Christ was born, that the cult of emperor worship really began. It must be said that Augustus did not accept the title of deity, but many of his subjects, particularly in the eastern part of the empire, considered him to be divine. Herod the Great rebuilt the city of Samaria, renaming it Sebaste, meaning "worthy of honor," to venerate Augustus. He built a great temple there, and dedicated it to the worship of the emperor, much to the disgust of the Jews. By the time of Emperor Caligula, who came to power within a decade after the death and resurrection of Christ, the leadership of Rome was openly seeking recognition as deity.

Actually, the worship of the emperor had an important political value, for it was a means of unifying the sprawling and diverse elements of the empire. At great public occasions it was quite impressive to see formal obeisance being done to the emperor as a kind of preliminary event before the race or the game. The people of that day looked on this practice with little more concern than we might do with regard to saluting our national flag. In a polytheistic age what was the worship of one more god? Most of the populace had their own local worship, most likely one of the popular mystery religions, so that the worship of the emperor was but a kind of political veneer, not really personal, and not taken too seriously.

In the first century one group did take this matter seriously. The Jews would not stoop to polytheism. They had been cured of idolatry by bitter judgment centuries before. The Romans were wise enough to know that they risked the mass revolution of a sizable portion of the population if they did not make special allowance for the unbending Jews. Therefore, the Jews, and the Jews alone, were given a special exemption from the worship of the emperor. This was a high tribute to the depth of the loyalty of the Jews to their religious tradition. An interesting sidelight of this is that during the decade of the A.D. sixties Christianity had become such a potent force in the empire that the Romans recognized that these disciples of Christ were not just another sect of the Jews but a distinct religious group. When this recognition came, the Christians no longer came under the special mantle of protection afforded the Jews, and the terrible era of Roman state persecution was ushered in, during which many thousands of faithful Christians lost their lives because they would not render worship to the state.

Summary

Greek philosophical systems, representing the most brilliant experiments in human reason, had failed to solve the problem of guilt and fear in the human heart. There was widespread disenchantment with the philosophies by the time of Jesus. It was a time of intellectual and spiritual bankruptcy. Attempting to fill the need for personal spiritual experience were the weird, sometimes fanatical, often immoral, mystery cults. These abounded in the days of Christ. As a veneer over the local pagan ritualistic religion was the emerging cult of emperor worship. Such was the world of pagan belief at the time that Jesus journeyed toward the cross.

Today there are many frustrated seekers who have tried many fountains but have come away still thirsting. May we who have tasted the water of life be faithful to share it with the spiritually thirsting!

9

The Early Years of Jesus

So the fullness of time came. We have ranged through the worlds of Judaism and paganism in an attempt to capture the setting upon which the greatest drama of the ages was to unfold. It is time now that we direct our attention to the central character. In the last two chapters of our study we shall journey with Jesus of Nazareth, from His early years through the turbulent days of public ministry, to the agony of the cross and the triumph of the empty tomb. As we trace the road of His life, let us remember with awe and wonder that because God became flesh and dwelt among men, becoming obedient even unto the death of the cross, conquering the greatest of enemies along the route, we as believers two thousand years later can revel in the sure knowledge of life eternal.

The Incarnation

It was about 4 B.C. The Emperor Augustus had called for a tax to be collected throughout his domains. In Palestine this required Joseph and Mary, living in Galilee, to journey to their tribal home in Judea, the town of Bethlehem. Mary was engaged to Joseph, according to the custom of the Jews. Yet a virgin, she was miraculously with child. To prepare this couple for the birth of the promised Messiah, God arranged for heavenly messengers to dispel their fears. An angel appeared to Joseph, reassuring him that what was conceived in Mary was indeed of the Holy Spirit, and that at the child's birth, His name should be Jesus, meaning "Jehovah is Deliverance" for

99

He would save men from sin (Matthew 1:18–21). During the sixth month of Elizabeth's pregnancy, the angel Gabriel had visited Mary at her home in Nazareth, giving a message similar to that given to Joseph (Luke 1:26–38). Now, at Bethlehem, Mary's time had come to be delivered. As if to symbolize the blindness of men, there was no room for the mother in the bustling community. In the warmth of an inn's stable, probably a cave, the Son of God was born. In the custom of the poor people of the land, the infant was wound about with strips of cloth, called "swaddling." The manger was probably a stone trough which served as a rather suitable makeshift bassinet. Later, like a papoose, the child was carried on the back of his mother, and slept at night in a wool cradle which swung between two poles.

In the Gospel narrative, there were three groups who recognized the infant as being Heaven's Ambassador. First, the shepherds on the Judean hills received the angelic announcement, and leaving their flocks, hastened to worship the King in His cradle (Luke 2:8–20). On the eighth day, according to the custom of the Jews, Jesus was circumcised (Luke 2:21). About a month later after having fulfilled the specified "days of purification" (outlined in Leviticus 12), Mary and Joseph journeyed to nearby Jerusalem to the Temple to dedicate the child, and to offer the prescribed Levitical sacrifice for her. It was while they were in the Temple that saintly Simeon and aged Anna perceived that the child carried by Joseph and Mary was the long-sought Messiah! Luke 2:25–39 records this delightful encounter. Would that all of us were as quick to respond to the gentle whispering of the Holy Spirit!

There was a third group who recognized the infant child Jesus as the King of kings. Sometime later, precisely how much later is not clear, the little family returned to Bethlehem where the Magi, or Wise Men, from the East came to pay homage. It is possible that Joseph intended to make Bethlehem a permanent home for it may have been many months after the birth of the child that the Magi arrived. High drama attended this visit, for in the encounter with the Wise Men who inquired regarding the whereabouts of the Child-king, Herod seized the information as a potential threat to his power. These mysterious men from the East responded to the warning provided through a dream, and after worshiping Jesus returned to their homeland without divulging the location of the child (Matthew 2:1–12). Now the sinister design of Herod was about to take shape. Every child in the vicinity of Bethlehem two years of age and under was murdered in this cruel attempt to snuff out a possible rival. However, Joseph had been warned of danger by an angel of the Lord who appeared to him in a dream, and in obedience to the warning, he took his little family to safety in Egypt (Matthew 2:13–15). How auspicious were these first events in the life of the One who had come to deliver man from the dominion of sin. The forces of evil were arrayed against Jesus from the beginning of His sojourn on earth.

At Home in Nazareth

In 4 B.C., the evil, half-mad King Herod died. Joseph made preparation to return to Bethlehem where he evidently planned to take up permanent residence. However, while the family was en route, they learned of the horrible bloodbath that had marked the inauguration of the new ruler, Archelaus, son of the deceased Herod. Thousands had been ruthlessly slain in an abortive revolt. Again God intervened, furnishing by means of a dream guidance for Joseph. Although it had not been part of his original plan, Joseph took the family along the seacoast, bypassing the vicinity of Jerusalem, eventually returning to Nazareth, 70 miles to the north in Galilee, far from the scene of terror (Matthew 2:19–23).

So it was that Jesus was to be called a Nazarene, for until the beginning of His public ministry at about the age of thirty He lived in Nazareth in the home of Joseph and Mary. Nazareth was quite unlike Bethlehem in Judea. Situated just a few miles to the southwest of the Sea of Galilee in a mountain valley, Nazareth was strategically located near an important intersection of trade routes. As a boy, Jesus no doubt saw caravans of exotic goods, fascinating and strange people from faraway places, and occasionally the marching Roman legions. Nazareth was a busy place. Perhaps because of its commercial character it assumed an evil reputation. "Can any good thing come out of Nazareth?" was the startled response of Nathaniel to Philip upon hearing the excited message that Jesus of Nazareth was truly the long-awaited Messiah (John 1:46). Galilee itself did not have a high reputation among the sophisticated in the center of Jewry, Jerusalem. Judea was more isolated from the bustling commercial traffic that flowed through the Near East; it was able to preserve its distinctive identity. Hence, the Judeans despised the inhabitants of the cosmopolitan "Galilee of the Gentiles," for there were so many Greek-speaking people there, and such a mixture of tongues and peoples, that the Galileans even had acquired a distinctive dialect loathsome to their southern neighbors (Matthew 26:73). Galilee was composed of rabble who butchered the mother tongue! And, Nazareth was one of the most wicked cities in that teeming, unsophisticated region. No, Jesus was not reared in guarded seclusion far from the rough and tumble of the masses of mankind. He was reared in the middle of jostling crowds, noise, and dirt. In accordance with the foreordained plan (Ephesians 1), Jesus came from heaven's throne to fully identify with mankind—and the most miserable of mankind—so that He could become a sympathetic and faithful High Priest to suffering humanity (Philippians 2:1–11; Hebrews 4:14–16).

"And the child grew, and waxed strong, filled with wisdom: and the grace of God was upon him" (Luke 2:40). "And Jesus advanced in wisdom and stature, and in favor with God and men" (Luke 2:52). A few short sentences is all the view the Gospel story gives us of the youth of Jesus. It is clear that Jesus grew in a normal manner appropriate to the Jewish lads of His time, reared in a strict, religious home, receiving the same kind of training, passing through the same varied experiences common to adolescents the world over. It is quite likely that Jesus found it necessary to shoulder the responsibilities of manhood somewhat earlier than most, for He, as Mary's eldest, seems to have had younger brothers and sisters. (John 7:5 indicates that there His "brethren" did not believe Him in the opening phase of His public ministry. Although the Semites tended to use terms of relationship, such as "brethren," more loosely than do we, the fact that James, Joseph, Simon, and Judas are listed as specific brothers, along with sisters [Matthew 13:55], provides a strong presumption for Jesus growing up with several half-brothers and half-sisters.) James and Jude later wrote the epistles named after them. Further, the fact that Joseph drops out of the story early seems to point to his dying a premature death, leaving a fatherless home. On the cross Jesus committed the care of His mother to the Apostle John, which suggests that Joseph was not alive (John 19:26, 27).

In the Jewish home, the mother bore the great responsibility for much of the early training of the children. Paul reminds young Timothy of the deep impressions that shaped his life which the loving care of grandmother and mother had provided (2 Timothy 1:5). So it must have been at the knee of Mary. But it was not left alone to the mother. Jewish tradition placed a solemn obligation upon the fathers to teach their sons the precepts of the Law. Scriptures, prayers, moral sayings—these were taught from the earliest moments in the deeply religious homes. The music of the Psalms filled the house, much as do gospel choruses in today's Christian homes.

When the boy was five or six years of age he was sent to the neighborhood synagogue school, where he sat on the floor in a semicircle with the other children, the teacher in their midst. Passersby could not help but hear the teaching process, for the basic method of instruction was loudly shouted repetition of sentences given by the teacher. Basic in the curriculum of the primary school was mastery of the Hebrew Scriptures, which was practically the only textbook until the child was ten years of age. The children were taught to read and write Hebrew, so that they could handle the Scriptures in the original tongue, although by the time of Christ the language of the streets was no longer classical Hebrew, but a Semitic dialect known as

Aramaic. The facility with which Jesus quoted the Hebrew Old Testament has led some to conclude that Joseph and Mary may have had the luxury of the Old Testament scrolls in their own home. The scribes maintained a careful scrutiny over the copying of the Scriptures, exercising most exacting care lest errors creep into the laboriously hand-copied manuscripts. Only with special permission were small, isolated passages of Scripture permitted to be copied by any other than the scribes themselves. This, of course, made the purchase of such scrolls an enormous expense, far out of reach of most. Not many but the most devout homes boasted their own copy of the Word of God.

As a boy, then, Jesus knew Aramaic, the vernacular of Palestine, and He without doubt spoke with the inflection common to Galilee. In addition Jesus knew Hebrew, for this He was taught in the synagogue school. Jesus may also have spoken Greek, for this was the commercial language of Galilee, and many inhabitants of the area were Greeks. Jesus was able to communicate with the Syrophoenician woman, who without doubt spoke Greek (Mark 7:26). It was not accidental that Jesus was reared in the most cosmopolitan province of Palestine, for it was in this manner that He was able to share deeply of the feelings and needs of diverse peoples from different cultures.

After the initial years of primary Bible instruction, at about the age of ten, the child passed on to a second level of instruction until approximately the age of fifteen. The subject matter in this program was the Mishna, or the rabbinical traditions that were already assuming a powerful influence by the time of Jesus. It is interesting that Jesus in His public ministry sharply distinguished between the divine authority of the Old Testament Scriptures and the traditions of men. Having studied such "traditions" as a youth, Jesus spoke with knowledge and conviction.

The curtain covering the early years of Jesus has not been drawn aside sufficiently for us to know whether Jesus passed on from the local synagogue schools to the academies operated by the most distinguished rabbis. At about the age of fifteen the most promising students were eligible for the more advanced rabbinical training, some even journeying to Jerusalem. We do, however, have one little vignette from the youth of Jesus. At the age of twelve Jesus accompanied Joseph and Mary to the Passover Feast in Jerusalem, which probably was the occasion of Jesus' becoming officially a responsible member of the Jewish religious community, or "bar mitzvah." It was here that this maturing youth disclosed an awareness of His unique mission, that He was the Messiah (Luke 2:41–51). However, He returned to live in subjection to the discipline of the home and family, spending His teen-age years and beyond in Nazareth, studying and working as a carpenter.

Summary

Jesus, the Son of God, was born into a devout, but simple home. His early years were lived in the dust and noise of a crossroads of the Near East, the wicked city of Nazareth. Here He developed insight and sympathy for Jew and Greek. In the plan of God the Messiah was fully identifying with man in need.

10

The Triumph of the Christ

Jesus was about thirty years of age when He entered upon His public ministry (Luke 3:23). Reckoning His birth to have occurred about 4 B.C., His years of preaching, teaching, and healing must have begun about A.D. 26, a judgment corroborated by other available extra-Biblical data. Assuming that the Gospel accounts of the life of Jesus are best harmonized around the chronology suggested by John, in which four successive Passover Feasts are mentioned, the public ministry of Jesus spanned three full years, culminating in the turbulent events leading to the Crucifixion, about the time of the Passover Feast of A.D. 29 or A.D. 30 (John 13:1). What makes the Christian message truly "Good News" is that death could not hold the Son of God! The empty tomb testified to the universe that the great objective of the coming of Jesus into this world had been successfully accomplished, the atonement at Calvary had indeed been declared to be efficacious for the sins of mankind. Let us follow the journey that took Jesus to the cross—and to triumph!

His Ministry Begins

John the Baptist. After four hundred years of virtual silence, again the prophetic ministry was heard in the land. God raised up John the Baptist to be the herald whose thundering message would indeed pave the way for the Messiah. "The voice of one crying in the wilderness, Prepare ye the way of the Lord, make his paths straight" (Matthew 3:3), a quotation from Isaiah of old, vividly described the Baptist. He had separated from the society of his day, living in the wilderness, clad in the rough garments of the typical prophet of earlier centuries, much like Elijah. His food was from the land. In fact, his life was a rebuke to the respectable Jewish world, a jarring and unsettling presence. Just how this wilderness evangelist attracted the throngs is not spelled out for us, but attract them he did, for "all Judea" went down into the rugged Jordan wilderness east of Jerusalem several miles away to hear this fascinating and bizarre preacher (Matthew 3:4–12). His message was fearless. He challenged the entire nation to repent. The Jews were deeply offended at the suggestion of baptism, for this was to them only for Gentiles who wished to become partakers in Judaism. What? Does that fellow think we are so sinful that *we* need to be baptized? It is interesting that John's baptism of repentance was once for all; it was not like the Essene ritual cleansing which was repeated daily.

In addition to the preaching of heartfelt repentance, John articulated with great boldness that the Kingdom was at hand. There was an urgency to his message. That a new era was dawning gave pungency and conviction to his challenge that the entire nation needed a baptism of repentance.

During the time that John had been gathering fame, one day Jesus joined the throng that journeyed into the wilderness. Suddenly, like a flash out of the sky, John singled out Jesus, and announced that the Messiah was standing among them, there in the crowd! "Behold the Lamb of God, that taketh away the sin of the world" (John 1:29). John objected to the insistence of Jesus that He be baptized by John, for John felt that Jesus did not need the baptism of repentance he had been proclaiming. However, not because He was repenting of sin, but that He might fulfill the will of God (Matthew 3:15), Jesus submitted to baptism. For Jesus this was the entrance into His public life; for John it was the culmination of his mission as a forerunner. Henceforth John would decrease that Jesus might increase (John 3:30), for the One for whom he had been preparing the way would baptize, not with water, but with the Holy Spirit!

At the time of the baptism of Jesus, the Spirit, like a dove, settled upon Him, and the voice of God beckoned the world to acknowledge His Son (Matthew 3:16, 17). A new era had begun.

The Wilderness Temptation. Immediately after the baptism at Jordan, Jesus was led by the Holy Spirit out into the wilderness, very likely into the rugged terrain of Judea, just west of Jordan. There He was subjected to the most terrible assaults that His adversary Satan could hurl at Him. Each of the temptations was a cunning attempt to get Jesus to bypass the central purpose of the Incarnation, His death on the cross. To turn stones into bread would have been the employment of His supernatural power for selfish gratification; to cast Himself down from a pinnacle of the Temple would have been recourse to gaudy display rather than the humility of the forthcoming cross; to obtain the kingdoms of the world by acknowledging the power of Satan would have been an easy, but hollow, route to power. Hungry, weary, alone, there Jesus battled with the forces of darkness. "It is written" was His repeated weapon (Matthew 4:1–11). Our victory, too, in the hour of temptation must be to stand on the sure Word of God! The victory won in the wilderness by Jesus disclosed His willingness, His determination, to journey resolutely, without wavering, all the way to Calvary. Now His ministry was about to begin.

The First Year: Obscurity

There is but the barest of information recorded in the Gospels during the first year of Jesus' ministry. What information is supplied comes from the Gospel of John, the Synoptics not furnishing any notice at all of that introductory year of ministry. That there is a high degree of selectivity in the writing of the biographies of Jesus by the Gospels' authors is quite understandable in the light of John 21:25: "And there are also many other things which Jesus did, the which if they should be written every one, I suppose that even the world itself would not contain the books that should be written." The purpose of the Evangelists is disclosed by John in the previous chapter: "Many other signs therefore did Jesus in the presence of the disciples, which are not written in this book; but these are written, that ye may believe that Jesus is the Christ, the Son of God; and that believing ye may have life in his name" (John 20:30, 31).

Immediately after the wilderness experience, Jesus returned to the site where John was ministering near the Jordan. His first mission was to call the first of the disciples. Two sets of brothers, Andrew and Peter, and Philip and Nathanael, were among the first to respond to the greatest of all invitations, "Follow me" (John 1:35–51). These evidently were some of John's followers who had been prepared for the Messiah, and whom John readily released to follow Jesus. Notice how absolute and decisive was their break with former associations; how complete was their response to the call of the Master! The growing aggregation of disciples came from a varied background, most of them lacking in the refinement and sophistication of the day, but they were teachable material in the hands of the greatest teacher of all, Jesus Christ. It would be on the foundation of ordinary men that the Church would be built, ordinary men who lived with Jesus for three years, and then retired to the Upper Room to be endued with the mighty power of the Holy Spirit. God is still enabling ordinary people for great service, ordinary people whose response to Him is absolute.

Shortly after the calling of the first disciples, Jesus and His little retinue made the journey northward from Judea to Galilee. Our next glimpse of Him is at Cana, a village not far from Nazareth. Here Jesus and His friends appear at a wedding feast, along with Mary. In the course of the merry festivities, the wine ran out, a terrible embarrassment to the master of ceremonies. The first of Jesus' miracles occurred here. The joy of the festive occasion was multiplied by the compassion of Jesus who turned many gallons of water into wine (John 2:1–11).

Jesus stayed briefly in nearby Capernaum, then returned southward to Judea to attend the Passover. With a blazing display of divine authority, Jesus invaded the Temple area, driving out the money changers and sellers of sacrificial animals, a priestly-controlled traffic. To Jesus this was sacrilege, a desecration of His Father's house (John 2:16).

During His brief stay in Jerusalem, numerous miracles were performed which attracted considerable attention (John 2:23). Among those so impressed was Nicodemus, an important citizen of the community, and a respected member of the Sanhedrin. The conversation between Jesus and this nighttime visitor is beautifully told in John 3. The challenge given Nicodemus is appropriate to all who wish to become disciples: "Ye must be born again." Those who would be Christ's followers must be born of the Spirit.

During the subsequent brief ministry in the countryside of Judea, many people came to see Jesus; so much so that some of John's loyal devotees became envious. Rather than allow discord to erupt, Jesus and His associates retired to Galilee (John 3:25 to 4:3). It was on this journey that Jesus encountered the Samaritan woman at the well near Sychar. Their journey to Galilee was delayed several days because of an unscheduled revival that broke out in Samaria (John 4:4–42). Jesus was still largely unknown when the first year of ministry came to an end in Galilee (John 4:43–45).

The Second Year: Popularity

Shortly after His arrival in Galilee, Jesus went to the synagogue in His hometown, Nazareth. The portion from the prophets for the day was from Isaiah 61. Jesus, as a visiting teacher, was invited to give an oral exhortation on the passage, a common custom. He boldly announced that He Himself was the fulfillment of that Messianic prophecy. The result was outrage by the local citizens. They were so angered by what they considered to be blasphemy that they sought to kill Him! Never again would Jesus be able to call Nazareth "home." The road to the cross was not easy (Luke 4:16–30).

In spite of the eruption in Nazareth, Jesus soon found a vast throng responding to His ministry throughout Galilee. Capernaum became His headquarters. Many there were healed on various occasions. The twelve disciples, whom He gave special apostolic authority, were all Galileans with the exception of Judas Iscariot who was a Judean. These were dispatched on a series of important missions, touring the region of Galilee (Matthew 10). His popularity was such that as many as five thousand heard Him on a single occasion (Mark 6:30–44).

In the midst of this lengthy Galilean phase of ministry, Jesus left briefly to attend the Passover in Jerusalem (John 5:1). The miraculous healing of a lame man on the Sabbath precipitated an unpleasant encounter with the Jews. So hostile were the Jews that they sought to kill Jesus (John 5:18). Aware that continued ministry in Judea was not opportune, Jesus returned again to Galilee, where His fame was abounding.

Not only did Jesus heal multitudes, but He taught them principles of the Kingdom, and preached that He was the entrance to the Kingdom. Matthew contains large sections of the teaching of Jesus, much of which was set forth in the Galilean countryside. Notable among these great discourses is the Sermon on the Mount (Matthew 5 to 7), very likely delivered among the low hills just west of the Sea of Galilee. His Kingdom is spiritual; not earthly. Judgment is coming, and only those who are properly related to Jesus will stand in the Day of Judgment (Matthew 7:21–23).

The Third Year: Opposition

The feeding of the five thousand was a major turning point in the popularity of Jesus. After a year of accelerating fame, the climax came with the spectacular multiplication of the loaves and fishes for the needs of the exuberant throng. At this point, however, Jesus began to speak in plain, forthright terms the true nature of His kingdom. His kingdom would be costly; His body must be broken. At the bewildering news that He would not be establishing an earthly monarchy, that He would not be organizing a revolution against Rome, the crowds melted away (John 6:66). So many who had just been fed by the miraculous bread and fish could not receive the teaching that

Jesus was the Living Bread which must be broken. Then in sorrow He turned to Peter and the rest of the twelve, saying, "Will ye also go away?" (John 6:67). For an additional six months or so, Jesus continued to minister in Galilee, but the mood of the crowds had changed. Finally, He turned southward, never again to see the scenes of His childhood and His great year of spectacular popularity. Galilee lay behind; the cross was yet ahead.

An important reason that Jesus had spent but brief sessions in Judea after the first months of public ministry was the wrath of the outraged religious leaders who dominated Jerusalem. As Jesus set out for Judea, without doubt He knew that the time of His death was imminent. Why were the religious leaders so violently opposed to Jesus? They objected to His novel interpretation of the Law, as if He had the right to penetrate the layers of rabbinical tradition heaped up through the centuries. He even proclaimed Himself to be lord of the Sabbath! (Mark 2:27, 28). His declaration that He was indeed the Son of God was considered by these blind leaders of the blind to be sheer blasphemy, a crime punishable by death. And, it could just be that His incisive, pungent critique of the hypocrisy and superficiality of their entire religious system produced intense conviction. He thus appeared as an ominous threat to their way of life, a threat that had to be done away with. So, as His public popularity evaporated in the face of His articulation of the terms of true discipleship, likewise, the organized ecclesiastical opposition in Jerusalem set about to destroy this irritating Galilean.

The lines were being drawn. By the use of parables Jesus drew to Himself those who really longed to know in fullness; the casually curious drifted back into their accustomed routines. A momentous occasion near the end of the Galilean ministry was the direct challenge of Jesus to Peter at Caesarea Philippi: "Who am I?" Peter, falling in worship before his Lord, cried out, "Thou art the Christ, the Son of the living God" (Matthew 16:13–17). From this point onward, Jesus spent more and more time instructing His closest followers, the Twelve, in the important matters concerning the Kingdom.

Perhaps it was but a few days later that Jesus was wonderfully transfigured before the faithful disciples, a scene hidden from the masses. There, in a blinding, dazzling, shining-through of His deity, the veil of His humanity was momentarily rent. Jesus in a preview of His coming glory disclosed for an instant that indeed He was the Son of God wrapped in flesh (Matthew 17:1–8). Noteworthy is the fact that such a privileged experience was not shared by any but the closest of His disciples. Just the inner circle, Peter, James, and John, were witnesses of that remarkable event.

Autumn was approaching. The Transfiguration apparently occurred while He was yet in Galilee. From thence He journeyed toward Jerusalem, sending seventy disciples to prepare the way in advance (Luke 10:1–16). During this period in the life of Jesus Luke places numerous of the beautiful parables, a characteristic of the teaching of Jesus at this time. These include the story of the Good Samaritan, the lost sheep, coin, and son, the importunate widow, and the unjust steward. Much of these last six months was actually spent across Jordan in Perea, for He knew that when He entered Jerusalem His life would be quickly ended. That last winter, in a strange, new area that He had not previously visited often, Jesus gathered new crowds, for His message and ministry blessed the throngs. Finally, in the spring He set His face toward Jerusalem. As He had done earlier in Galilee, He turned to the cheering throngs, stilling their exuberance with the call to total commitment, spelling out with unmistakable precision the demands of discipleship (Luke 14:25–35). Jesus was preparing the great throng for the ordeal that would come within the week. And so few really got the message!

When Jesus crossed the Jordan to enter Judea for the final confrontation with the religious leaders of Jerusalem, He made His home at nearby Bethany, just a short distance east of the city. There was that delightful resting-place, the nearest thing to home that Jesus enjoyed in Judea, where Mary, Martha, and

Lazarus lived. The crowning miracle of the ministry of Jesus occurred there. Lazarus, already in the tomb four days, was raised from the dead (John 11:17–44). Jesus had proven His mastery over disease, demons, storms, and even death itself! But, this last, climactic miracle also brought to the boiling point the fanatical hatred of the Jewish leaders, for the wonder of Jesus was threatening the hold they had on the people (John 11:45–54).

The Triumph of the Cross

Palm Sunday was the open declaration to the world that Jesus was the Messiah. What a day of acclaim and rejoicing! It was in truth a triumphal entry. Riding on an ass's colt, the symbol of royalty to that culture, Jesus came in preview-fashion as King of kings (Matthew 20:29 to 21:11). Upon arriving at the Temple area, Jesus cleansed the Temple for the second time, driving out those who profaned the Court of the Gentiles with their greed (Matthew 21:12–17).

Each evening of that week Jesus retired to Bethany, coming to Jerusalem during the day. His days were filled with encounters with scribes and Pharisees. Remarkable prophecies about the destruction of the Temple, and of His own second coming, punctuated His utterances.

Meanwhile, the plot against His life was germinating. On Thursday evening, immediately after the Last Supper (John 13 to 17), the little band of disciples retired to the Garden of Gethsemane. Following that mighty prayer of final resolution, Jesus in a great agony of soul drank the bitter cup (Matthew 26:36–44). Judas, in league with the Sanhedrin, entered the garden, and betrayed Jesus with that treacherous kiss. During that long night, Jesus was spirited from religious court to civil court, a trial filled with mockery of their own Jewish law.

In the morning Jesus, unjustly condemned, was turned over to the Roman soldiers to be beaten, mocked, and finally made to carry His own cross outside the city walls to the place of execution. There He hung, like a vile criminal, between two thieves. Late in the afternoon, Jesus gave up His life. A centurion standing by cried out, "Surely this man was the Son of God!" (Mark 15:39). Joseph of Arimathea and Nicodemus took down the body, prepared it for burial, and laid it in a rock tomb, at which was placed a special guard (Matthew 27:62–66).

What the Jewish leaders had thought to be the final vanquishing of the Galilean was in fact a triumph of the Messiah they could never quite understand. On Sunday morning, that first Easter Day, sorrowing disciples were jarred by the announcement that Jesus had risen from the dead! And, for 40 glorious days, the glorified Christ continued to appear to His disciples throughout the land. The Resurrection demonstrated that the atonement at Calvary had been full satisfaction for our sins.

Now, Jesus carefully pointed out to His overjoyed disciples that although He must go away for a time, He would come again. And, in the meantime, all His faithful followers were to tarry in Jerusalem and to await the promised Comforter, the blessed Holy Spirit, who would be with them to the very end, empowering them to take the good news that JESUS SAVES to the ends of the earth!

Summary

The love that Jesus displayed in His earthly sojourn has been the pattern, the ideal for His disciples through the centuries. His teaching never grows dull, for it is meat and drink to the thirsting soul. But, it is His death, the triumph of the Cross, that makes possible forgiveness by a Holy God whom we have grievously offended. The curse of divine wrath fell on Jesus instead of us. And, the Resurrection announces that the Great Sacrifice was indeed acceptable in the court of heaven.

If Jesus came into a real world, to deal with real problems, to die for people just like us, should we not bow in wonder and worship? Should we not invite Jesus of Nazareth to be Lord of our lives? That mighty conqueror who towered over His times stands quietly, patiently, to hear our response.

Books for Further Study

BOUQUET, A. C. *Everyday Life in New Testament Times.* New York: Charles Scribner's Sons, 1953.

CROSS, FRANK M., JR. *The Ancient Library of Qumran and Modern Biblical Studies.* Garden City, New York: Doubleday and Company, 1961.

EDERSHEIM, ALFRED. *The Life and Times of Jesus the Messiah,* 2 vols. New York: Longmans, Green, and Company, 1883.

FAIRWEATHER, WILLIAM. *From the Exile to the Advent.* Edinburgh: T. and T. Clark, Fifth ed., 1894.

GIFT, JOSEPH L. *Life and Customs in Jesus' Time.* Cincinnati: The Standard Publishing Foundation, 1957.

MACKIE, G. M. *Bible Manners and Customs.* New York: Fleming H. Revell, n.d.

METZGER, BRUCE M. *The New Testament: Its Background, Growth, and Content.* New York: Abingdon Press, 1965.

PFEIFFER, CHARLES F. *Baker's Bible Atlas.* Grand Rapids: Baker Book House, 1961.

PFEIFFER, ROBERT H. *History of New Testament Times.* New York: Harper and Brothers, 1949.

ROBERTSON, A. T. *A Harmony of the Gospels.* New York: Harper and Brothers, 1922.

STALKER, JAMES. *The Life of Christ.* New York: Fleming H. Revell Company, 1891.

TENNEY, M. C. *New Testament Times.* Grand Rapids: William B. Eerdmans Publishing Company, 1965.